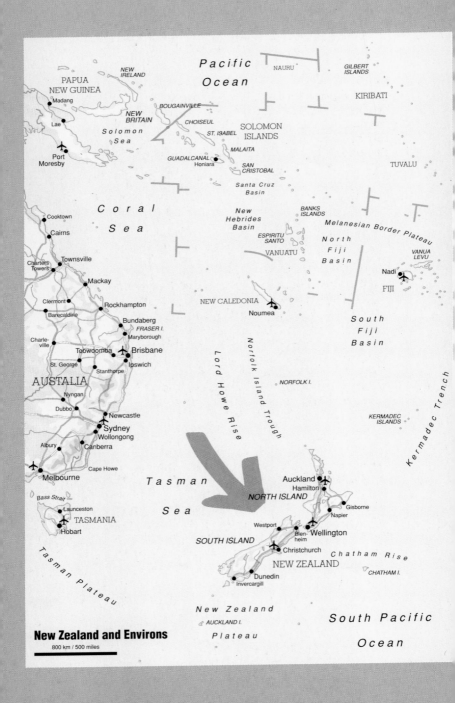

New Zealand and Environs

800 km / 500 miles

INSIGHT *Pocket* GUIDES

New Zealand

KIWI

the pride of the pacific

APA PUBLICATIONS

Dear Visitor!

New Zealand is a unique and wonderful country – its geography is dramatic and expansive, its population is small, but welcoming and friendly. From the sub-tropical climate of the north to the temperate south, from golden sand beaches washed by sparkling seas to grand fiords fringed by dense rainforests, from glaciers carving through rugged mountains to wide plains of fertile farmland, and from cosmopolitan cities to small towns, New Zealand is indeed a 'different down under', worthy of your attention.

 Craig Dowling, our correspondent, was born and bred in New Zealand and has seen the country grow from under the umbrella of the British Commonwealth to a Pacific nation ready and willing to assert itself on the world stage. He has lived and worked as a journalist in the country's three largest cities – Auckland, Wellington and Christchurch – gaining a broad insight into the diversity that makes New Zealand such a special place. 'There is so much to see and do right down the entire length of the country,' he says. 'So much variety, in fact, that the most difficult job for any visitor is not in deciding what to do, but in deciding what not to do.'

Dowling brings a keen sense of enthusiasm and a love of his country to this book, using his extensive local knowledge to make easy those tough decisions that face travellers to New Zealand. He brings the country to life with a background into its history and culture and guides you to some of the best attractions on offer. Dowling makes travelling in New Zealand a cinch with well-crafted itineraries that span the North and South islands, taking in the main tourist hubs of Auckland, Rotorua, Wellington, Christchurch and Queenstown and also to places beyond. As they say in Maori, the language of the indigenous people of New Zealand, 'Haere Mai' – Welcome!

Hans Höfer
Publisher, Insight Guides

C O N T E N T S

Pages 2/3:
Milford Sound
with Mitre Peak in
the background

*Pages 8/9:
The neo-Gothic
Christchurch
Cathedral*

HISTORY

A joke which is occasionally directed at New Zealand and New Zealanders goes: 'What is the difference between a New Zealander and yoghurt?' Answer: 'Yoghurt has a culture'. The reason for the joke is not hard to see because New Zealand does lack some of the trappings of history and culture that manifest themselves in the art galleries, museums and castles familiar to Europe.

The only answer to this criticism is that New Zealand is, well, New Zealand. It was settled by Europeans often attempting to escape the restraints of Britain, most notably its rigid class-based society. This desire is manifested in what became known as the 'Great New Zealand Knocking Machine' – a Kiwi tradition of criticising people who try to distinguish themselves too much from the rest.

Despite this, New Zealand has managed to cultivate its fair share of the fine arts. For artists like Colin McCahon (1919–1987), Gordon Walters and Jane Evans, recognition is hard won in a country where sport is accorded the status of a religion. Nevertheless, New Zealand's artists continue to create in crisp bright hues and with freshness, drawing on a mixture of colonial and indigenous influences. New Zealand has its writers too, like Booker Prize winner Keri Hulme, Janet Frame and Witi Ihimaera. And it has its music and its musicians, ranging from symphony orchestras to hip rock bands like Crowded House.

Old Arts Building, Auckland

In terms of social movements, New Zealand has been influenced by forces from Western Europe (especially UK) and the US, adopting ideas and turning them into action with often more vigour than the countries of their birth. In late last century for instance, New

Culture

Zealand was the first country to grant universal suffrage to women. Amidst the economic pressures of the first half of this century, New Zealand developed one of the most advanced systems of social welfare for its people. And the trend has continued. While laissez-faire economic policies took a foothold in the UK and the US in the 1980s, New Zealand set about dismantling unwieldy government establishments with more determination than either, to the extent that the country is being watched as a test case by analysts in the 1990s.

Whether the changes have been good or bad, it serves to illustrate a common feature of New Zealanders. If a job has to be done, there will be someone prepared to do it. This, and an easy going attitude – encapsulated in the common Kiwi phrase 'she'll be right' – partly explain the number of New Zealanders who have distinguished themselves on the world stage; people like Sir Ernest Rutherford, the Nobel prize-winning physicist who theorised about splitting the atom; Sir Edmund Hillary, who conquered Mount Everest; and Dame Kiri Te Kanawa, the great opera diva.

Kiwi culture goes beyond Maori arts and crafts

The Lonely Islands

The level of achievement is quite startling, given the fact that the country's population hovers around the 3.4 million mark. And it is even more startling when you look at the relatively short time span that New Zealand has existed as a nation.

For the greatest part of its existence, New Zealand has been un-inhabited by land mammals, aside from two species of bat. For

The kiwi some 100 million years up until perhaps only the last 1,000 years, New Zealand developed in isolation from every-where and everything but the forces of nature.

It was forested by large native conifers such as the kauri. Ancient animals looming in the undergrowth in-cluded reptiles like the tuatara, large ground snails, and, in the absence of predators, several native bird species – the two most famous examples being the small kiwi, and the huge but now extinct moa – who, lacking the need, lost the ability to fly. They were joined on the ground by flightless insects like the large weta. Seeds, travelling on winds and wings to the islands brought a diversity to the flora that is a distinct feature of New Zealand to this day.

First Footsteps

And then came the human factor – but not for thousands of years. Indications are that a gradual migration into the Western Pacific some 4,000 years ago led first to the development of the distinctive Polynesian culture, and ultimately to the first human footprints be-ing made in about the 10th century, on the islands which were called Aotearoa.

By the 12th century, settlements were scattered over most of the country. And having had few or no continuing contacts with the outside world, these settlements developed unique characteristics now recognised as Maori culture.

The Maori developed a com-munal society based on groups of varying sizes, ranging from the extended family grouping, or *whanau* (pronounced 'far-now'), to large tribes, or *iwi* (pro-nounced 'ee-we'). Tribes were or-ganised around a chief (*rangatira*) while family groupings were headed by elders (*kaumatua*). Maori livelihood was ensured by the subsistence farming of root crops such as the delicious sweet potato (*kumara*), and supple-mented by fishing, hunting and plant gathering.

Inter-tribal warfare was a com-

A tatooed Maori rangatira (chief)

A pa (fortified village)

mon feature of life, though not on a huge scale. However, when the growing population put pressure on the asset most prized by Maori – the land – a system of fortified villages (*pa*) was developed. Although often warlike, there was a lot more to the early Maori. The *pa*, for example, often featured buildings with elaborately carved facades; and art, music, dance and an oral literary tradition reached a high level of refinement.

It has been estimated that there were more than 100,000 New Zealanders, all Maori, living in New Zealand during the late 18th century. All but a few thousand lived in the North Island. One book summarised their situation thus: 'Fiercely protective of their social identities, they were deeply attached to the land which gave them physical and spiritual life. Their ways of living had evolved many local variations. They had no concepts of nationhood or race; and as they began to encounter Europeans, they saw them as members of another, if stranger, rival tribe.'

More Company

The first recorded visit to the land of Aotearoa by Europeans came in December 1642 when Dutch explorer Abel Tasman sighted the west coast of the South Island. It was an inauspicious discovery. Abel Tasman proved himself not very able by initially naming the sighting Staten Landt, mistaking it for part of South America. He mapped a small stretch of the coast, but was attacked by Maori while anchoring near what is now known as Golden Bay (he called it 'Murderers' Bay'). He left without setting foot on the land.

That inauspicious beginning may have been partly to blame for the hiatus in European exploration of the region, for it was not until 1769 that British explorer Captain James Cook advanced knowledge of New Zealand. Captain Cook circumnavigated the country, and his charts and journals made the land known to the outside world. Indeed, he took a fancy to the land himself, returning there for two more visits, in 1773–74 and 1777.

In the late 1700s and early 1800s, New Zealand developed as an offshoot of New South Wales in Australia. A chaplain to the New South Wales Penal Colony, Rev Samuel Marsden, set up the first mission station in New Zealand in 1814; about the same time when whalers made landings and set up stations on the New Zealand coast.

The mountain named after Cook

Colonisation

Progressively, other settlements were established, and European crops and cropping methods were introduced to the Maori. Their reactions varied, to say the least. Some Maori were happy to comply in order to obtain the strange gifts (often blankets and muskets) of the *pakeha* (white settlers). Others were antagonistic. And still many more were ambivalent. Indeed it is true to say that in 1840, when British sovereignty was proclaimed over New Zealand, there were many inland Maori who had still never met a *pakeha*.

The pace of white settlement quickened after sovereignty was declared, with a rush for land led by the New Zealand Company.

In 1852, a General Assembly was established by the British Constitution Act. However, the protection supposedly offered to the Maori in the 1840 signing of the Treaty of Waitangi failed to materialise. Land was bought for often inadequate prices, traditional Maori values were undermined and *pakeha* diseases proved virulent to a native population with little or no developed immunity. This led to a series of clashes known as the New Zealand Wars in the 1860s. The outcome was inconclusive which resulted in the further dispiriting of the Maori population and the increased momentum in the process of colonisation.

The medal for gallantry, NZ Wars

The discovery of gold in the rivers of the central South Island led to an economic boom for the European settlers while the subsequent development of technology to ship frozen meat to Britain further established a platform for New Zealand's growth.

Wide-ranging social reforms took place in the 1880s, and in 1893, New Zealand became the first country in the world where women could vote in the national elections. A system of old age welfare pensions was also introduced, giving New Zealand a reputation as 'the social laboratory of the world.'

The Twentieth Century

New Zealand moved from the status of a colony to a Dominion (a self-governing territory) of the British Empire in 1907, but strong loyalist links saw tens of thousands of New Zealand soldiers serve the Allied cause in World War I. New Zealand soldiers distinguished themselves but in no place more than during the ill-fated

Gallipoli Campaign. ANZAC Day on April 25, commemorating the lives lost in that battle, is now a public holiday in New Zealand, and Gallipoli is seen as an important event in the development of the nation's patriotic identity.

New Zealand suffered with everyone else in the depression of the 1930s. Bloody unemployment riots took place and disenchantment led to the election of the first Labour Government in 1935. By 1936, New Zealand's non-Maori population had grown to almost 1½ million, with distinct movements both northwards and into the cities. The Maori population had stabilized after being severely hit during an influenza pandemic in 1918 and hovered around the 60,000 mark. Land grievances were still a burning issue but the forum for debate had shifted into parliament. Influential Maori politicians who fought the Maori cause include Sir Peter Buck, Hone Heke and Sir Apirana Ngata.

World War II again saw Kiwi soldiers fighting alongside the Allies. But significant changes were set in motion at this time. Firstly, the war stimulated a redirection of the country's trade to non-British markets. Secondly, post-war immigration from war-ravaged Europe coupled with a 'baby-boom' considerably boosted the country's population.

The post-war period can be divided into two distinct phases. An initial one of prosperity and near full employment, followed by a period of forced reappraisal of the country's position in the world. The event which shook New Zealand most was the entry of Britain into the European Economic Community and its undertaking to buy meat and dairy products from other EEC members. New Zealand was suddenly faced with the disappearance of the major export market for its major export – agricultural products.

The trauma that this caused New Zealand was very real. But it also provided the impetus for New Zealand to forge ahead.

NZ's meat industry suffered when Britain joined the EEC

New Zealand Today

The country today is considerably more economically diverse than it was 30 years ago. The infrastructure is more balanced between primary, tertiary and secondary industries and there is an awareness of New

Patriotic New Zealanders

Zealand being a Pacific country with a Pacific culture.

Close economic ties have been established with Australia and politically, New Zealand is becoming much more involved in world affairs on its own terms. The people of New Zealand have taken a strong moral stand on nuclear and environmental issues, to the extent that they create an impact on the Pacific region. Invariably, this has led to areas of conflict with powers such as the US and France. The ANZUS Treaty between New Zealand, Australia and the US was effectively 'put on hold' after New Zealand refused a visit by an American nuclear-powered warship. And a Greenpeace Vessel, the *Rainbow Warrior*, which was on its way to protest against French nuclear testing on a Pacific atoll, was bombed by French agents in Kiwi waters.

This has led to a country less naive than perhaps it once was. There is a realisation that New Zealand is no longer a country isolated from the rest of the world. And it is revelling in this fact. In recent years, it has lobbied for, and won a seat on the United Nations Security Council. And as a further example of its more outward approach, New Zealand's Tourism Board is in the process of actively seeking to treble the number of visitors to the country by the year 2000.

If you are one of those attracted to New Zealand you will find that some things, thankfully, have not changed. Firstly, there is the inherent beauty of the country. And secondly, there is the charm of the people. Innocence may be on the way out, but it is not lost, and is still more easily found in New Zealand than most other places in the world – yoghurt or no yoghurt.

The bustling Auckland waterfront

Historical Highlights

1000 Arrival of first Polynesian settlers.

1642 European discovery by Abel Tasman.

1769 Capt James Cook's first exploration of New Zealand.

1814 Rev Samuel Marsden establishes Anglican mission station.

1826 Attempt at European settlement under Capt Herd.

1840 Arrival of New Zealand Company's settlers. New Zealand annexed by New South Wales. Capt Hobson appointed Lieutenant-Governor. Treaty of Waitangi is signed.

1841 New Zealand proclaimed independent of New South Wales.

1845 'Northern War' between Maori and *pakeha*.

1852 Constitution Act passed. New Zealand divided into six provinces.

1854 First session of the General Assembly in Auckland.

1858 Te Wherowhero becomes Maori 'King'.

1860 'Taranaki War' between *pakeha* and Maori.

1861 Gold discovery in Otago. First electric telegraph line opened.

1863 First steam railway in New Zealand.

1865 Seat of Government transferred to Wellington.

1870 First rugby match in New Zealand. Last battles of 'New Zealand Wars'.

1876 Provincial governments are abolished.

1882 First shipment of frozen meat from New Zealand.

1886 Tarawera volcanic eruption. Pink and White Terraces destroyed.

1893 Universal female suffrage is introduced.

1907 New Zealand granted Dominion status.

1908 North Island main trunk railway opened. Ernest Rutherford awarded Nobel Prize in Chemistry.

1914–18 World War I. Gallipoli campaign by ANZAC troops.

1918 Influenza epidemic.

1931 Hawkes Bay earthquake.

1935 First New Zealand Labour Government elected.

1939–45 World War II. New Zealand Division serves in Italy.

1947 Statute of Westminster adopted by parliament.

1949 National Government elected.

1951 Prolonged waterfront industrial dispute. New Zealand signs ANZUS Treaty alliance with United States and Australia.

1953 Sir Edmund Hillary climbs Mount Everest.

1962 Western Samoa becomes independent.

1965 Cook Islands become self-governing. Combat troops sent to Vietnam.

1967 Decimal system introduced.

1972 Labour Government elected.

1974 Commonwealth Games hosted in Christchurch.

1975 Waitangi Tribunal established to hear Maori land rights issues. National Government elected.

1981 Tour of New Zealand by South African rugby team leads to riots.

1983 Signing of Closer Economic Relations Agreement (CER) with Australia.

1984 Labour Government elected on anti-nuclear platform. Embarks on economic reform programme.

1985 Greenpeace protest vessel *Rainbow Warrior* bombed by French agents in New Zealand.

1986 Goods and Services Tax (GST) introduced.

1987 Non-nuclear legislation becomes law. Power of Waitangi Tribunal extended.

1990 Commonwealth Games hosted in Auckland. National Party wins general election.

1993 Signing of 'Sealord Deal' giving Maori interests ownership of major fishing company. General election. National Government returned with slim majority. Vote to change electoral system to a proportional system called MMP.

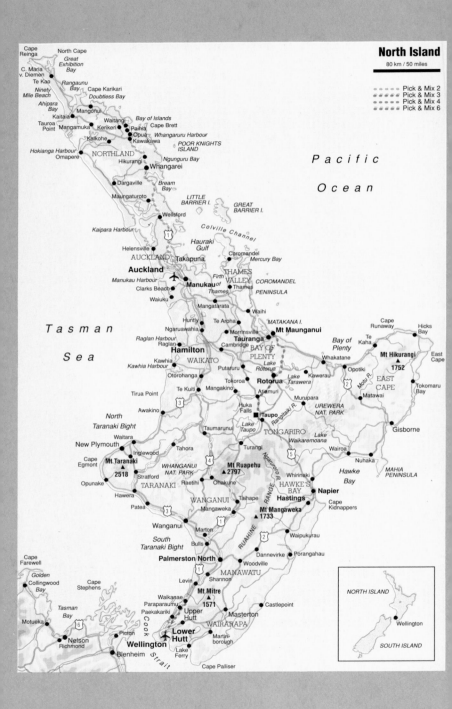

North Island

80 km / 50 miles

- Pick & Mix 2
- Pick & Mix 3
- Pick & Mix 4
- Pick & Mix 6

Cape Reinga
North Cape
Great Exhibition Bay
C. Maria v. Diemen
Te Kao
Rangaunu Bay
Cape Karikari
Ninety Mile Beach
Doubtless Bay
Ahipara Bay
Kaitaia
Mangonui
Tauroa Point
Waitangi
Cape Brett
Mangamuka
Kerikeri
Paihia
Bay of Islands
Kaikohe
Opua
Whangaruru Harbour
Kawakawa
POOR KNIGHTS ISLAND
Hokianga Harbour
Omapere
Hikurangi
NORTHLAND
Ngunguru Bay
Whangarei
Dargaville
Bream Bay
Maungaturoto
LITTLE BARRIER I.
GREAT BARRIER I.
Wellsford
Kaipara Harbour
Colville Channel
Helensville
Hauraki Gulf
AUCKLAND
Takapuna
Coromandel
Mercury Bay
Auckland
THAMES VALLEY
Manukau Harbour
Manukau
of
Thames
COROMANDEL PENINSULA
Clarks Beach
Thames
Waiuku
Mangatarata
Waihi
Huntly
Te Aroha
MATAKANA I.
Ngaruawahia
Morrinsville
Tauranga
Cape Runaway
Hicks Bay
Raglan Harbour
Cambridge
Mt Maunganui
Te Kaha
Raglan
Hamilton
BAY OF PLENTY
Bay of Plenty
Whakatane
Mt Hikurangi
Kawhia
WAIKATO
Lake Rotorua
1752
East Cape
Kawhia Harbour
Putaruru
Opotiki
EAST CAPE
Otorohanga
Tokoroa
Lake Tarawera
Kawerau
Motu R.
Tirua Point
Te Kuiti
Mangakino
Rotorua
Tokomaru Bay
Atiamuri
Awakino
Huka Falls
Murupara
Matawai
North Taranaki Bight
Taumarunui
Taupo
UREWERA NAT. PARK
Waitara
Lake Taupo
Gisborne
New Plymouth
Tahora
TONGARIRO
Lake Waikaremoana
Inglewood
Turangi
Wairoa
Cape Egmont
Mt Taranaki
Nuhaka
MAHIA PENINSULA
2518
WHANGANUI NAT. PARK
Mt Ruapehu
Whirinaki
Opunake
Stratford
Raetihi
Ohakune
HAWKE'S BAY
Hawke Bay
Hawera
TARANAKI
Taihape
Napier
Patea
WANGANUI
Mangaweka
Hastings
Mangaweka
Mt Mangaweka
Cape Kidnappers
Wanganui
Marton
1733
Waipukurau
South Taranaki Bight
Bulls
Dannevirke
Porangahau
Cape Farewell
Palmerston North
Woodville
Golden Bay
MANAWATU
Collingwood
Cape Stephens
Levin
Shannon
Tasman Bay
Waikanae
Mt Mitre
Castlepoint
Paraparaumu
1571
Motueka
Paekakariki
Upper Hutt
Masterton
Nelson
Picton
WAIRARAPA
Richmond
Lower Hutt
Martinborough
Wellington
Blenheim
Lake Ferry
Cape Palliser

P a c i f i c

O c e a n

T a s m a n

S e a

RUAHINE RANGE

Rangitaiki R.

Waioeka R.

Cook Strait

NORTH ISLAND

Wellington

SOUTH ISLAND

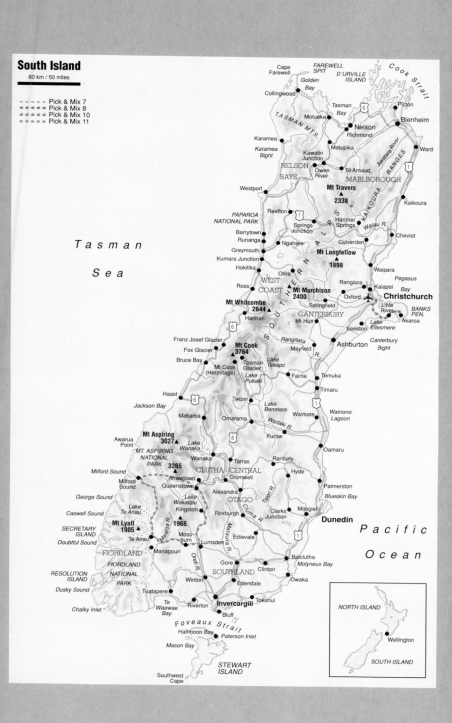

South Island

80 km / 50 miles

- - - - Pick & Mix 7
- - - - Pick & Mix 8
- - - - Pick & Mix 10
- - - - Pick & Mix 11

Tasman

Sea

Cape Farewell
FAREWELL SPIT
D'URVILLE ISLAND
Cook Strait
Golden Bay
Collingwood
Tasman Bay
Picton
Motueka
Blenheim
Nelson
Richmond
Ward

Karamea
Kawatiri Junction
Matupika
TASMAN MTS.
Karamea Bight
NELSON BAYS
Owen River
St Arnaud
MARLBOROUGH
Awatere River
KAIKOURA RANGES

Westport
Mt Travers 2338
Kaikoura

Reefton
PAPAROA NATIONAL PARK
Springs Junction
Hanmer Springs
Waiau R.
Cheviot
Barrytown
Culverden
Runanga
Ngahere
Greymouth
Mt Longfellow 1898
Kumara Junction
Hokitika
Waipara
Otira
Rangiora
Pegasus Bay
Ross
WEST COAST
Mt Murchison 2400
Kaiapoi
Oxford
Christchurch
Mt Whitcombe 2644
Springfield
Little River
BANKS PEN.
Harihari
CANTERBURY
Mt Hutt
Lake Ellesmere
Akaroa
Leeston

Franz Josef Glacier
Mt Cook 3764
Rangitata
Ashburton
Canterbury Bight
Fox Glacier
Mayfield
Bruce Bay
Tasman Glacier
Lake Tekapo
Mt Cook (Hermitage)
Lake Pukaki
Fairlie
Temuka
Haast
Timaru
Jackson Bay
Twizel
Lake Benmore
Waimate
Wainono Lagoon
Makaroa
Omarama
Waitaki R.
Awarua Point
Mt Aspiring 3027
Lake Wanaka
Kurow
MT. ASPIRING NATIONAL PARK
Oamaru
3265
Wanaka
Tarras
Milford Sound
Arrowtown
CLUTHA · CENTRAL
Ranfurly
Milford Sound
Queenstown
Cromwell
Hyde
George Sound
Lake Wakatipu
Alexandra
OTAGO
Palmerston
Caswell Sound
Kingston
Roxburgh
Blueskin Bay
Lake Te Anau
Clarks Junction
Mosgiel
SECRETARY ISLAND
Mt Lyall 1905
Clutha R.
Dunedin
Doubtful Sound
1968
Te Anau
Mataura R.
Mossburn
Edievale
FIORDLAND
Manapouri
Lumsden
RESOLUTION ISLAND
FIORDLAND NATIONAL PARK
Oreti R.
Balclutha
Dusky Sound
Gore
Molyneux Bay
SOUTHLAND
Clinton
Chalky Inlet
Winton
Edendale
Owaka
Tuatapere
Te Waewae Bay
Riverton
Tokanui
Invercargill
Bluff
Foveaux Strait
Halfmoon Bay
Paterson Inlet
Mason Bay
STEWART ISLAND
Southwest Cape

Pacific

Ocean

NORTH ISLAND
Wellington
SOUTH ISLAND

Introduction

New Zealand's geography, while providing scenes of unsurpassed beauty, poses some difficulties for the independent traveller. There is an abundance of diversity in the landscape, but New Zealand is long and thin, rough hewn and split into two main islands, making travelling time often longer than you expect. The bottom-line is that when your vacation time is short, it is impossible to see everything the country has to offer.

This is where *Insight Pocket Guide: New Zealand* can help you. This selection of itineraries is designed to introduce you quickly, and efficiently to the best New Zealand has to offer.

NORTHLAND
OLDEST SETTLEMENTS
LONGEST BEACH
MILDEST CLIMATE
BIGGEST TREES

For this purpose, the itineraries focus on five main hubs – chosen because of the range of attractions they offer, and their easy accessibility. These hubs are: Auckland, whose international airport is the country's principal gateway; Rotorua, a hot springs wonderland in the central North Island; Wellington, New Zealand's capital city; Christchurch, the South Island's principal gateway; and Queenstown, the beautiful lakeside resort area in the lower part of the South Island.

Full-day, mainly walking itineraries guide you to the best of each of these hubs. In addition to these, a selection of *Pick & Mix* options have been included. These range from tours of a few hours to longer day trips which get you away from the hubs, to see some of the glory and diversity of the outlying countryside. If you have the time, many of the options can be extended into overnight stays.

For these itineraries the assumption is made that you will have access to a car, and that you will be linking the hubs by internal flights, if time is a premium, and by car, if it is not. Based on this premise, the rest of the planning is up to you. However, I have these words of advice: travel to at least one hub in each of the main islands and for every two hubs you visit, indulge in at least one of the *Pick & Mix* options.

If you are in New Zealand for just a few days, or a week, this guide is invaluable. Of course I would advise you to stay longer. If you do, the itineraries can be strung together for an extensive South to North, or North to South tour of the whole country.

Within these extremes, the possibilities are endless and you will be left with a valuable insight into this fascinating land, and the life of New Zealanders.

AUCKLAND

DAY 1

A full-day walking itinerary (by car if the weather is inclement) taking in Queen Street, the Auckland Domain and War Memorial Museum, Parnell, Albert Park and the Auckland City Art Gallery.

Auckland is New Zealand's largest city, containing within its urban sprawl more than a quarter of the country's entire population. What draws people here, as it has for centuries, is the combination of warm sub-tropical climate and the bountiful twin harbours of Waitemata and Manukau. Between the two harbours is an isthmus dotted with extinct volcanoes. Founded by European settlers in 1840, Auckland was the seat of Government for a time until Wellington took over in 1865.

Begin your tour from the **Auckland Visitor Centre** (Tel: 366 6888, Monday to Friday 8.30am–5.30pm, weekends and public holidays 9am–5pm), situated mid-way up Auckland's main drag, **Queen Street**. There is public parking available beneath Aotea Square, accessed off Mayoral Drive. The Centre is a good place to pick up maps and gather more information about Auckland and its surroundings.

Aotea Square, just out the door of the Visitor Centre, has several points of interest for the traveller. The first is the **Waharoa** (gateway), elaborately carved as a symbolic entrance to the square and in stark contrast to the mirrored glass buildings and the modern bustle

Queen Street

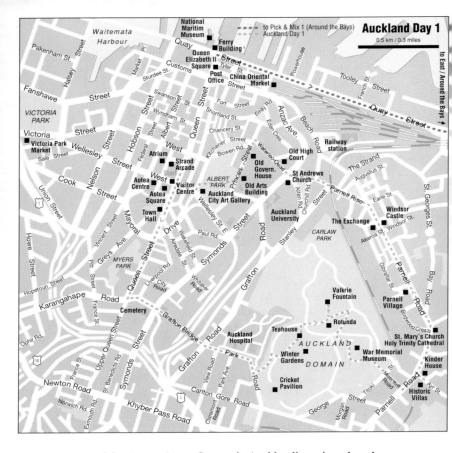

around it. Across Aotea Square is Auckland's main cultural venue, the **Aotea Centre**. Walk across and browse in the foyer to see if the centre is hosting any events of interest to you.

From the Aotea Centre walk out to Queen Street and turn right, up the rise. At the top of Queen Street is the intersection with **Karangahape Road**. Never mind if you have trouble with the pronunciation; most of the locals do too, and just call it K-Road. But be warned that you may get some knowing glances asking directions to this road because of its reputation. Around to the right about 500m (547yds) away are a series of seedy strip-joints. The area is safe by day, but is best avoided at night. You should go left at K-Road instead, past some small shops, the remnants of the city's original cemetery, and straight on across Grafton Bridge, with its views over the city's skyline.

Walk along what is now Park Road and about 400m (437yds) beyond the bridge. Just past the main Auckland Hospital entrance is an entrance to the inner-city sanctuary known as the **Auckland Domain**. Walk down the sign-posted road.

The Domain was the site of a huge volcanic explosion which took place thousands of years ago, leaving features on the landscape still visible today. The wide crater has formed a natural amphitheatre

arching from the hospital to the War Memorial Museum.

Looking right, between the pine trees as you head into the Domain, you will see the old **Cricket Pavilion**. The grandstand was built in the early 1900s, replacing an original one destroyed by fire in 1887. This part of the Domain, as well as being the venue for cricket, is the site for many cultural activities.

Walk on down the road and then cut inland against the flow of the cars (if you are driving, continue around on the longer route to the first carpark and join the itinerary at the Wintergarden Teahouse). Just 20m (22yds) along is an oasis of lush foliage and a fountained pond.

On your right you will come to a glass atrium and the **Winter Gardens** (open daily 10am–4pm), which houses some 10,000 exotic plants. After a brief ramble around, rest your feet at the charming **Wintergarden Teahouse** to the left of the road. The Teahouse (open daily 9am–5pm) is a wonderful place for morning tea, and I heartily recommend the three-tiered tea stand laden with goodies.

Suitably repasted, follow the path in front of the tearooms leading around the pond to a carpark. On your left is a map and useful information on the Domain. Use the map to guide you past the Watson Bequest Statuary. To your left as you walk east is the **Formal Gardens** (spectacular in summer months) that lead down to the **Valkrie Fountain**. The fountain sits at the bottom end of a flower-filled roundabout about 100m (109yds) off the road. Between the bushes you can see out and over the Waitemata Harbour to the volcanic cone of Rangitoto Island.

Return to the road, heading east past the band rotunda and a statue honouring Scottish bard Robert Burns (1759–96). From here you should be able to see, on a crest, the dramatic **Auckland War Memorial Museum**, opened in 1929 (Tel: 377 3932, open daily 10am–5pm, admission free). The steps of the museum offer another wonderful platform from which to view Auckland. Walk right around the museum for a panoramic view of the city's landmarks, including the distinctive **One Tree Hill**.

The museum itself has an extensive range of displays, but for the first time visitor to New Zealand, it is most valuable for the superb introduction to Maori culture. See artefacts such as a raised storehouse, a carved meeting house and, possibly the most spectacular exhibit, **Te Toki Tapiri**,

Auckland War Memorial Museum

the last of the great Maori war canoes, whose hull was carved out of a single Totara log. The 25-m (85-ft) long canoe, built in 1836 could carry some 100 warriors. **Pounamu Ventures** (Tel: 836 7876) run morning and afternoon guided tours of the exhibits and I recommend you join one.

Leave the museum by heading south (away from the harbour) on the road that passes the Parnell Tennis Club on your left. Walk straight out across Titoki Street and along Maunsell Road about 400m (437yds) and you come to Parnell Road. Turn left and head towards **Parnell**. This is one of the oldest areas of Auckland and the restored villas make it a worthwhile visit.

Parnell Village

But first, venture into **Ayr Street**, the first on your right, for two historic villas open to the public: **Kinder House** (2 Ayr Street, open daily 10.30am–4pm) offers afternoon teas in the former residence of a 19th-century painter, while **Ewelme Cottage** (14 Ayr Street, Tel: 379 0202, open daily 10.30am–noon and 1–4.30pm) was built back in 1863.

Back onto Parnell Road you soon come to **St Mary's Church**, regarded as one of the finest wooden Gothic buildings in the world, and the new **Holy Trinity Cathedral**.

Just 30m (33yds) on you come to the corner with St Stephens Avenue, the top end of Parnell Road. You are greeted by a mixture of old style bakeries, 'dairies' (small grocery stores), fish and chip shops, and the start of the designer shops which become more apparent just a little further down.

The **Parnell Village** complex, just beyond Birdwood Crescent on the left side of Parnell Road, is a shopping mecca made from a collection of wooden villas reclaimed and beautifully restored. It makes a charming diversion from your stroll. Explore the myriad of shops, head out back and amble around the verandas, and over the little bridges linking villa to villa.

Lunch stops here include **Konditorei Boss** (305 Parnell Road), a popular German pastry shop and cafe in the Parnell Village complex and the **Metropole** (223 Parnell Road) wine bar. If the Auckland humidity is starting to get to you, have a beer at the **Windsor Castle**, a traditional style Kiwi pub on the right hand side of Parnell Road on the corner with Akaroa Street, or the more up-market **The Exchange** on the left hand side.

After lunch, walk down Parnell Road and veer left down Parnell Rise heading back into the city centre. When you get to the bottom of the rise, take a deep breath because you are now going up the other side again. A path leads from Churchill Road up through a reserve area to the Symonds Street/Alten Road intersection and the Presbyterian church of **St Andrews** with its large Romanesque columns. Opposite the church is a low fence signalling the lower grounds of Auckland University.

Cross over, heading west along Waterloo Quadrant and you will see the **High Court** on your right, with its historic older chamber and court rooms joined to a modern extension. Work started on the old Court building in 1865 and the first sitting took place three years later. The arresting carved stone heads and gargoyles which adorn the exterior of the court were crafted by Anton Teutenburg, a Prussian immigrant who was paid 15 shillings a day for the task. If you call the High Court (Tel: 309 8836) you may be able to arrange a tour. Otherwise, there is a public gallery from where you can watch legal proceedings. At the **QC's Coffee Bar**, just near the Old Court entrance, they do justice to a good afternoon tea.

Moving on, the **Old Government House** (12 Princes Street) is on your left. Cross the road to the entrance and take a stroll through the grounds, now owned by the univer-

Albert Park

sity. Walk along beside the building and enjoy some of the dense gardens on the hillside leading up to Princes Street.

Make your way up to Princes Street, dominated by the **Old Arts Building**, which was designed and built by Auckland University College and opened in 1926. Look inside the front door to the immaculately tiled entrance hall.

Opposite the Old Arts Building is **Albert Park**, a beautifully maintained inner city sanctum featuring a floral clock, statues of Queen Victoria and Sir George Grey (1812–98, a strong and influential early leader of colonial New Zealand), band rotunda and hordes of students lazing on the grass – occasionally even with books!

Take one of the paths on the western side of the park that lead downhill to Kitchener Street, and on the southern corner with Wellesley Street you will find the **Auckland City Art Gallery** (Tel: 307 7700, open daily 10am–4.50pm, admission free). This was New Zealand's first permanent art gallery when it was opened in 1888. It also houses one of the country's best collections of New Zealand and European art.

Drop down Wellesley Street just a short distance away and you are back in the heart of Auckland – Queen Street.

Turn right and, if you have the energy, spend the rest of the afternoon exploring the delights of Auckland's inner-city shopping. Watch out for the historic **Strand Arcade** (233–237 Queen Street) and the newer shopping precinct, **the Atrium**, on Elliott Street, and the end of the Strand Arcade. Duty free shopping is concentrated towards the lower end of Queen Street.

PICK & MIX

1. Around the Bays

Travel along Tamaki Drive around Auckland's spectacular waterfront. Visit Kelly Tarlton's Antarctic Encounter and Underwater World and take in views of the Waitemata Harbour. Lunch at Mission Bay and continue to Archilles Point. Half-, or a full-day if you decide to linger at the beaches along the way.

Auckland's dominant feature is its sparkling harbour – the Waitemata – and this itinerary gives you a fabulous opportunity to experience it. Start from the **Downtown Ferry Building** at the bottom of Queen Street. Visit the adjacent **Hobson Wharf** featuring New Zealand's **National Maritime Museum** (Tel: 358 1019, open daily 10am–5pm with extended hours in summer) before heading east along Quay Street, keeping the port on your left.

If you are travelling with children, or are feeling mischievous yourself, head for **Lilliput** (Tel: 524 4096, open daily 10am–10pm), a small theme park a little further along on your right at the start of Hobson Bay.

As you drive along what is now **Tamaki Drive**, the volcanic cone of **Rangitoto Island**

Ferry Building

looms large across **Waitemata Harbour** to your left. Rangitoto means 'blood-red' sky and the island's summit is 260m (854ft) high. It can be visited by ferry (Fullers Cruise Centre, Tel: 367 9111), and an easy track leads to the crater rim. The island is administered as a wildlife sanctuary and sustains a wide variety of native flora and fauna.

Contrasting with Rangitoto's natural serenity is the human influence all along State Highway (SH)77. Views of the harbour are highly sought after and the houses here command premium prices. Following the route, with signposts to St Heliers, you will pass the first of many city beaches along the way, this one being **Okahu Bay**. On your right is the extensive grassed area of **Orakei Domain**.

As you drive on around the bay, watch out for **Hammerhead Restaurant**, a large eatery

Auckland waterfront

Face to face with 'Jaws'

on your right. Use it as a landmark to move into the right-hand lane and ease off the accelerator as just beyond the restaurant, turning across the traffic, is the scene of your first leg-stretch: **Kelly Tarlton's Antarctic Encounter and Underwater World** (23 Tamaki Drive, Tel: 528 0603, open daily 9am–9pm).

When it was opened in 1985, Kelly Tarlton's was the first aquarium of its type in the world. Built under the sea, special acrylic tunnels take you through holding tanks of exotic New Zealand marine life. The complex was recently expanded to include a journey in special 'snow cats' for a taste of the Antarctica wilds. The heated vehicles plunge through a fierce whiteout storm to emerge in the tranquil beauty of a recreated Antarctic landscape. You could easily spend an hour in each section of Kelly Tarlton's.

About 400m (437yds) further along Tamaki Drive is a turn-off right for Bastion Point and the **Michael Joseph Savage Gardens and Memorial** (gates close at 9.30pm during summer and at 8pm in winter). Head up the road to the parking area at the top and a great view back to the city and over the harbour.

Michael Joseph Savage (1872–1940), the memorial to whom stands guard over the point, was the first Labour Prime Minister of New Zealand. The land behind the memorial is open grazing land, unusual amidst the suburbia of Auckland, and was the scene of a major Maori land rights protest in the 1970s.

After your fill of fresh air, history and scenery, follow the road back out to Tamaki Drive, turn right again, and soon you arrive at **Mission Bay**. If in search of sustenance, this is the place to get it. Park either in the carpark at the far end of the beach, or on your left past the large clock. For coffee and a light snack, try **The Cafe** (85 Tamaki Drive, Mission Bay, Tel: 528 5026), decorated in distinctive black and white. Alternatively, have a picnic on the lawn leading to the beach with supplies gleaned from across the road at **Butlers on the Bay** (55 Tamaki Drive).

Take a walk along the promenade, settle yourself on the sand, or paddle in the sea. When time or curiosity finally gets the better of you, find your car again and continue on along Tamaki Drive past **Kohimarama Beach**, and then **St Heliers Bay**, lined with more golden sand and frequented by older people. By driving to the end of Tamaki Drive and taking Cliff Road you come to **Archilles Point Reserve**, with its commemorative plaque in honour of HMS *Archilles* which took part in the 1939 Battle of the River Plate. Wander to the look-out point 20m (22yds) away for more photo opportunities of the harbour.

From here, either retrace your steps to any particular site that took your fancy, or take a rather complicated inland route back through some quiet Auckland suburbia. To achieve the latter, follow the cycle route signs for about 7km (4½ miles) past Churchill Park and through Glendowie. Take a right from Roberta Drive into West Tamaki Road. Follow this to St Heliers Bay Road and turn left before dropping down Kohimarama Road (Route 6). Keep veering right and you will ultimately end up back on Tamaki Drive near Hobson Bay. Left takes you back to the centre of town, with the round trip to the Ferry building being no more than about 32km (20 miles).

2. Bay of Islands

Head away early on this full day trip north of Auckland as it requires a lot of driving. If you have the time, stay overnight at the Bay and spread the sightseeing over 2 days. Take SH1 up through Warkworth and Whangarei to Paihia. Visit the historic Waitangi Treaty House and cross by ferry to Russell. Return to Auckland via the Waiwera Hot Pools.

The **Bay of Islands**, 241km (150 miles) north of Auckland, is an area of notable firsts in New Zealand's history. It was the legendary

Aerial view of Bay of Islands

landing place of Polynesian explorer Kupe in the 10th century; Captain Cook sheltered in the bays and gave the area its current name in 1769; New Zealand's first European colonists settled in Russell; the Treaty of Waitangi, New Zealand's founding document was signed here; Russell was the nation's first capital. The list goes on.

But first you have to get up early to enjoy it. Leave at about 7am as the drive north can take up to 5 hours, depending on traffic and stops en route. To head out of Auckland, drive west along Quay Street at the bottom of Queen Street and follow the signs over the Harbour Bridge. Continue on along SH1 north, following the signs to Whangarei.

A good breakfast spot is **Warkworth**, just under an hour from Auckland in an area known as the **Kowhai Coast**. It is a beautiful small town on the Mahurangi River and is worth a trip on its own if you don't have time to make the full journey to the Bay. Try the **Bridge House Lodge** (Tel: 425 8351) on Elizabeth Street by the bridge for breakfast, and stretch your legs with a walk by the river.

A further drive of just over 100km (62 miles) will bring you to Northland's main city, **Whangarei**. An information centre on your left on SH1 (Tarewa Park) as you enter the city has good facilities including tearooms. Follow the signs to Kawakawa, which you should reach in about an hour from Whangarei, and then look for the turn-off to Paihia via Opua.

There are a plethora of things to do in **Paihia**, especially in summer but be warned, the beautiful bays, beaches and history combine to make the area a tourist magnet.

Check with the **Bay of Islands Information Office** (Maritime Building, Tel: 402 7426, open daily 8am–6pm) upon arrival to plan your day. There are several boat trips offered around the islands, including the famous Cream Trip, and trips to 'The Hole in the Rock'. These can be done if you're staying overnight. If you are only there for the day, take a ferry to **Russell**. Once known as 'the hell hole of the Pacific' and famous for its unruly population of whalers and runaways, it is now a quiet town with a distinct Victorian atmosphere. Walk the waterfront and hunt out New Zealand's first industrial building, **Pompallier House**.

Waitangi Treaty House and Haruru Falls

Return to Paihia by mid-afternoon for a visit to the **Waitangi National Reserve** (Tel: 402 7437, open daily 9am–5pm). Allow at least an hour to stroll the grounds, visit the Maori meeting house, view the magnificent Maori war canoe and see **Waitangi Treaty House**, where the historic document was signed in 1840.

Returning from the Reserve, you should visit the fascinating **Kelly Tarlton's Museum of Shipwrecks** (Tel: 402 7018, open daily 10am–10pm) on board the ship *Tui*. Then go for a drive to the pretty **Haruru Falls**, turning right after the bridge coming back from the reserve.

To round off the day with a nice dinner, drive back through Paihia to Opua and sample the seafood at the moderately-priced **Ferryman's Licensed Restaurant** (Tel: 402 7575, open daily for dinner from 6pm).

The **Anchorage Motel** (Tel: 505 100) on the Paihia waterfront, and the **Waitangi Resort Hotel** (Tel: 402 7411) in the Waitangi National Trust grounds are two mid-range options for accommodation if you decide to stay the night. Otherwise, when heading back to Auckland, I recommend you make a diversion at **Waiwera Hot Pools**, 47km (29 miles) north of the city, and relax those tired driving muscles with a soak in the hot mineral pools (Tel: 426 5369, open daily 9.30am–10pm). They are pure bliss.

ROTORUA

DAY 1

Rainbow Farm to Lake Tarawera

A full-day driving and walking itinerary. Begin with a short drive up SH5 to the Skyline Gondola for a view over Rotorua. Visit Rainbow Springs and Rainbow Farm before taking a paddle-steamer cruise on the Lakeland Queen. Visit the Whakarewarewa Thermal Area and take a scenic drive to the Blue and Green Lakes. See the Buried Village, then return to Rotorua for a dip at the Polynesian Pools. Round off the night with a Maori concert party and a hangi meal.

Rotorua, as the locals proudly boast, is the only place in New Zealand where you can tell exactly where you are with your eyes closed. They are referring, of course, to the distinctive aroma of sulphur that permeates the town, courtesy of its boiling mud pools and hot springs. To visit Rotorua with your eyes shut would be a travesty, however, because it is an area of rich cultural and scenic beauty. Block your nose, and head out boldly.

Your day begins at the **Tourism Rotorua Travel and Information Office** at 67 Fenton Street (Tel: 348 5179, open daily 8am–5pm). Pick up useful information and maps from the office, and book ahead for a variety of activities and accommodation.

Leave at about 9am, or else you may have to sacrifice the 10.30am farm show at Rainbow Farm later on. Head west on Arawa Street then turn right onto Ranolf Street (the start of SH5). The drive takes you past **Kuirau Park** on your left, a 25-ha (62-acre) reserve; good for an evening stroll. Drive on, and along Fairy Springs Road (still SH5) about

Maori carving, Rotorua

4½ km (3 miles) out from the city, aiming for the **Skyline Skyrides** gondola (Tel: 347 0027, open daily 9am–9pm).

The Skyline is on your left and there is ample parking, so pull off the road, buy a ticket and in a matter of minutes the 900-m (2,953-ft) lift, with a vertical rise of 200m (656ft) takes you up the slopes of Mt Ngongotaha for a panoramic view. Stroll around and gaze over the region you will soon be exploring.

Half an hour or so and it's time to ride back down either on the gondola or the 1-km (½ mile) long luge, or slide ride. If you have some time you may want to walk around **Hillside Herbs**, a herb garden next to the carpark. Admission is free but do not dawdle. Just 100m (110yds) down the road is **Rainbow Farm** on your right (Tel: 347 8104) and Rainbow Springs on your left (Tel: 347 9301). Park by the springs and follow the signs leading you under the road to the farm. Every day

Let's see your teeth – Rainbow Farm Show

at 10.30am (and also at 11.45am, 1pm and 2.30pm), a special show introduces visitors to New Zealand's farming heritage. Efficient farm lads take you through the finer points of mustering, shearing, and a range of other farm activities. The admission also includes entry to the next attraction on your itinerary, the Rainbow Springs.

After strolling around the farm viewing new-born farm animals and a kiwifruit display, take the path back under the road to your next Rotorua experience. **Rainbow Springs** (open daily 8am–5pm) boasts more than 150 species of native New Zealand fauna spread over picturesque grounds. Join up with a guide who will introduce you to pools of clear water alive with rainbow and brown trout.

The pools are linked via a stream to Lake Rotorua, with the fish free to come and go as they please. Some 6,000 fish – who know when they are on to a good thing – hang around to watch visitors.

It takes between 1 and 2 hours to tour Rainbow Springs. Then, follow SH5 back towards town and take the turn-off for Lake Road and the lakeside. Park the car in the ample lakefront parking area near the jetty. Every day at 12.30pm the *Lakeland Queen*, a 22-m (72-ft) paddlesteamer carries passengers around Lake Rotorua on a lunchtime cruise. Catch it if you can (Tel: 348 6634, reservations essential). On board, you will be entertained with the love story of Hinemoa and Tutanekai – a Maori legend of Romeo and Juliet proportions, but with a happy ending.

If you miss the boat, or choose not to sail, 50m (55yds) to your left (facing the lake) is the **Lakeside Cafe and Crafts Shop** (Tel: 349 2626). Have lunch here and check out the selection of crafts.

You can, and should, also walk north-west from the cafe along the narrow driveway that heads past the **Rotorua Yacht Club** around the lakefront to **St Faith's Church** and **Ohinemutu**. This tiny village on the lake-front was the main settlement when the first

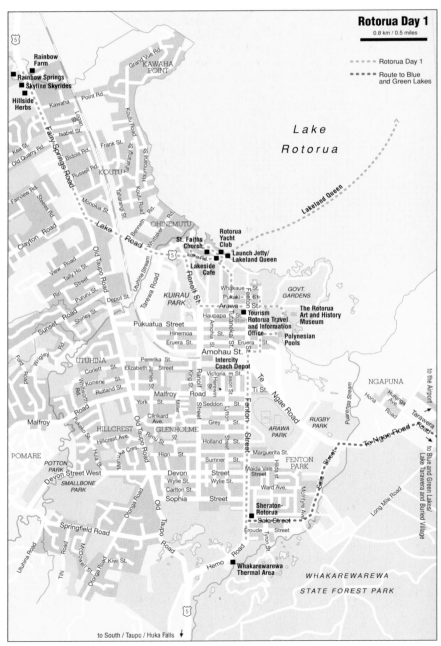

Rotorua Day 1

0.8 km / 0.5 miles

- - - - Rotorua Day 1
●●●● Route to Blue and Green Lakes

Europeans arrived last century. The settlement is famous for a rather glum bust of Queen Victoria, presented to the community in thanks for the local tribe's support during land wars. But there is also St Faith's Church, built in 1910. A curious feature is the raised graves around the church, made necessary by the thermal activity beneath the ground. Take a look at the beautiful window within St Faith's, where the placement of the Maori Christ, with the lake as a backdrop, creates an illusion of the statue walking on water.

After strolling the lakefront, return to your car and head for a quick look at the downtown shopping. Leading directly south from the park area at the lakefront is **Tutanekai Street**, Rotorua's main drag. There are a wide variety of shops, though not particularly spectacular, and more eating options. Parking is easy to find all along the street. Return to your car and drive east on Whakaue, Pukaki or Arawa streets, all of which take you to **Hinemaru Street** and the **Government Gardens**. Park on Hinemaru Street and walk through the gardens.

Rotorua Art & Hist Museum

Within the grounds, **The Rotorua Art and History Museum** (Tel: 349 8334, open weekdays and public holidays 10am–4.30pm, weekends 1–4.30pm) is well worth a visit. The distinctive Tudor-style building built in 1908 is home to artefacts from Rotorua's past and recounts the romantic history of the famous Pink and White Terraces (which you will see later in this itinerary) and also the history of the Te Arawa tribe.

Sometime now you should practice trying to pronounce the name of your next destination – **Whakarewarewa** (say Fok-a-ray-wa-ray-wa). To get there, turn right at the south end of Hinemaru Street into Amohau Street and then the first left turn into Fenton Street. Just 1½ km (1 mile) down the road on your left is the **Whakarewarewa Thermal Area** (Tel: 348 9047, open daily 9am–5pm). The closest thermal resort to the city, though arguably not the most spectacular, it has the added attraction of the **New Zealand Maori Arts and Crafts Institute** within its gates. The area has extensive and varied thermal activity ranging from bubbling mud pools and boiling springs to the famous **Pohutu Geyser** which erupts up to a height of 30m (98ft). Allow at least 1½ hours to explore this area and the time-warp **Whakarewarewa Living Village**.

From Whakarewarewa, it is scenic drive time as you head for the mysterious **Green and Blue Lakes**. To get there, drive back up Fenton Street towards town, turn right into Sala Street just by the Sheraton Hotel, follow the street out to Te Ngae Road (SH30) and then turn off on the first main road to your right – Tarawera

Sliding into Blue Lake

Road. About 10km (6 miles) from the city, along the forest-fringed Tarawera Road, you suddenly drop down to the beautiful sight of Tikitapu, or the **Blue Lake**. The broad pumice-sand beach is divided into swimming and water-skiing areas, while a wide grassy verge is ideal for picnics. The sight itself is breathtaking, with the dark-blue water stretching out to meet the green bush-clad hills. Have a dip in the lake. Or else, hire a canoe or pedal boat from the Blue Lake Holiday Park just up behind the road.

Continuing on, the road rises to a crest and a vantage point from which you see both Tikitapu, the Blue Lake, and the larger Rotokakahi, the **Green Lake**. This lake is not open for boating or swimming however, because it is *tapu* (sacred) to local Maori. The road instead swings down around the edge of the lake, but gives you no access to the water.

Here you are following the historic tourist route opened last century to the former **Pink and White Terraces**, once known as the eighth wonder of the world. The naturally-formed silica terraces on the shores of **Lake Rotomahana** were like a giant staircase, with a fan-shaped edge spilling across almost 300m (328yds) of lakefront. But nature proved unkind to its own wonders, and now people follow the route to witness a tragedy. For on 10 June 1886, the massive volcanic eruption of Mount Tarawera obliterated the terraces and destroyed two Maori villages by burying them under a hail of ash and mud. Enormous devastation was also wreaked elsewhere.

A memorial to the tragedy is just a few minutes' drive past the Green Lake – the **Buried Village** excavations of Te Wairoa (Tarawera Road, Tel: 362 8287). A marked walk takes you through the village excavations and sites including a Maori *whare* (house), a flour mill, blacksmith's shop, a store and a hotel. Soak in the surreal atmosphere of the village, watched over by the legacy of the early European settlers – poplar and sycamore trees. Watch out for the *whare* where a Maori elder, who had foretold the tragedy, was trapped for four days before being rescued alive.

Another interesting exhibit is the front third of a large canoe believed to have been constructed by northern tribes for an attack on Te Arawa at Rotorua in 1823. Depending on time, and energy level, you can either make your way back to the entrance of the Buried Village, or take the longer route back via the waterfalls and caves. The latter route is not easy, but it is rewarding, leading you through native bush to the **Te Wairoa Falls**. After the uphill climb that ends the track you will be ready for afternoon tea at the Buried Village's tea rooms.

From Te Wairoa, it is a short drive further along the same main road to **Lake Tarawera**. You will first come to a lookout point, with Mount Tarawera looming across the lake in the distance. Then drop down to the waterfront and the Tarawera Landing, situated at a quiet little bay with a jetty. In the summer you may be able to join a late afternoon cruise on the MV *Rere Moana*, operated by **Lake Tarawera Launch Cruises** (Tel: 362 8595, departs daily at 1.30pm, 2.30pm, 3.30pm and 4.30pm).

The invigorating Polynesian Pools

Time to return to Rotorua. Follow the same route back out along Tarawera Road to Te Ngae Road which leads you back to Fenton Street. To round off the evening, have a dip in the **Polynesian Pools** (Tel: 348 1328, open daily 6am–10pm). Turn right, off Fenton Street, into Eruera Street or Hinemoa Street. The eight outdoor pools with pumice floors and water from the Priest and Radium Springs are the perfect elixir to a busy day.

Top off the night with a **Maori Hangi** and cultural show. These are held at several of Rotorua's top hotels, including the **Quality Resort Lake Rotorua** (Fenton Street, Tel: 348 1234) and the **Sheraton Rotorua** (Fenton Street, Tel: 348 7139). A *hangi* is the traditional Maori method of cooking food. Pork and vegetables are buried in the ground on top of red-hot stones that steam-cook the food for hours. Join in the concert and you may finish the night with a Maori *hongi* – a pressing of noses to signify friendship.

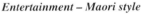

Entertainment – Maori style

PICK & MIX

3. Taupo

An easy-paced day or half-day trip from Rotorua, heading south on SH5 to Huka Falls and Taupo. Cruise on New Zealand's largest lake and return via the Craters of the Moon.

Taupo the town is sited on the shores of Lake Taupo, New Zealand's largest lake. Located just 90km (56 miles) south of Rotorua along a picturesque route featuring the famous Huka Falls, Taupo makes a worthwhile half- or full-day excursion.

Follow Fenton Street south an onto SH5 – the route to Taupo. About 20km (12½ miles) south of Rotorua you will pass the turn-off to **Waimangu Thermal Valley** (Tel: 366 6137, open daily 8.30am–5pm), a hot-bed of activity that was created in the 1886 eruption of Mount Tarawera. Attractions include **Waimangu Cauldron** and the colourfully named **Inferno Crater** and **Ruamomko's Throat**.

Back onto the SH5 and further 10km (6 miles) south you will

Bubbling Champagne Pool, Waiotapu

pass the **Waiotapu Thermal Wonderland** turn-off (Tel: 366 6333, open daily 9am–5pm). Waiotapu is famous for the **Lady Knox Geyser** which blows its top at 10.15am each day, and the boiling **Champagne Pool**. If you are doing this itinerary as a half-day excursion, it's worth coming here and paying a nominal fee just to see Lady Knox .

SH5 joins with SH1 just 2km (1¼ miles) short of Wairakei; beyond that, about 72km (45 miles) from Rotorua is the turn-off to the Huka Falls Tourist Loop Road. Take this road and call in first at the **Honey Village** (open daily 9am–5pm, admission free), marked by the yellow and brown painted VW Beetle. At the village – actually just a barn – get an insight into the production of honey and sample the local produce.

Just 2km (1¼ miles) along the road is the Wairakei Park and the Huka Falls carpark. A short walk takes you to views of the thundering **Huka Falls**, at the upper reaches of New Zealand's longest river, the Waikato.

The raging Huka Falls

If you follow the tracks that lead along the banks of the raging river you may also get a glimpse of the exclusive **Huka Lodge** (Tel: 378 5791). The secluded and luxurious fishing and hunting lodge, accessed from the Huka Falls Road (or, more frequently, by helicopter) has played host to many of the world's rich and famous, and has established a formidable reputation for itself as one of the finest private lodges in the Southern Hemisphere.

Further on the loop road you will come to the historic **Huka Village** (open daily 9am–5pm), a re-creation of an old colonial town. The **Poplars Cafe** within the village is ideal for morning tea.

A lookout point just at the end of Huka Falls Road, beyond the Huka Village, gives you a panoramic view of Taupo. Dropping down SH1 into Taupo you will find the **Information Centre** on the main thoroughfare, **Tongariro Street**, just back from the lakefront.

While in Taupo, walk along the lakefront and choose between the myriad of activities on offer. Highly recommended is a cruise on the **Ernest Kemp**, a replica 1920 steamer built in 1980 (Tel: 378 3218). Eric Dittmer runs the cruises with daily departures at 10am and 2pm from the wharf at the western end of Lake Terrace. He is full of the history of Lake Taupo and will take you to the Maori carvings on a rockface accessible only by boat.

For lunch, try the Hollywood-themed **Hudders** restaurant (22 Tuwharetoa Street, Tel: 378 5919, open noon–10pm), or if you are in town in December or January, the moderately-priced but elegant **Truffles** restaurant, housed in a beautifully restored cottage (116 Lake Terrace, Tel: 378 7856).

Just 5km (3 miles) back up SH1 on the return trip to Rotorua is the turn-off to the **Craters of the Moon** (open daily 9am–5pm), another eerie thermal landscape, steaming rather than exploding, with free entry and interesting walks.

Lake Taupo in a quiet mood

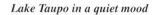

A day or half-day drive north of Rotorua through the kiwifruit growing area of Te Puke to Mount Maunganui. A picnic at the beach and on to Tauranga.

The Tauranga district, like Taupo, is an easy day trip from Rotorua. Alternatively, if you want to turn it into a scenic drive, it can be done in half a day. This itinerary takes you through forests and fertile kiwifruit growing areas of the **Bay of Plenty** to two relaxed coastal settlements, **Tauranga** and **Mount Maunganui**.

The drive from Rotorua is just 86km (53½ miles) along an interesting north-bound route. Follow SH30 out of town (Te Ngae Road, left off Fenton Street as you head away from the lake) which circles around Lake Rotorua and takes you past the airport. Ignore the turn-off to Hells Gate Thermal Area, continuing around the lake on what is now SH33. The highway veers inland away from the top end of Lake Rotorua and sweeps past Okawa Bay, providing some picturesque views of Lake Rotoiti.

A little further on watch out for signs to **Okere Falls**. Take the sharp left turn just past the Okere Falls shop and follow the signs to a small carpark. This option takes you to the start of an easy 10-minute walk to a lookout directly above the Kaituna River.

Continuing on by car from Okere Falls and about 50km (31 miles) from Rotorua (just before Paengaroa), watch for signs to **Longridge Park** (Tel: 533 1515, open daily 9am–5pm). The park is a unique attraction combining a relaxed drive-through farm-setting, cafe, a kiwifruit plantation and thrilling jetboat rides on the upper reaches of the Kaituna River. After Longridge and Paengaroa, you join up with SH2 leading through **Te Puke**. About 6km (4 miles) east of town you will see a giant slice of kiwifruit marking **Kiwifruit Country** (open daily 9am–5pm), another tourist attraction with kiwifruit as the theme. If you are passing by around lunchtime, Kiwifruit Country has a very good restaurant.

A roundabout signals the approach of Tauranga and Mount Maunganui. Do not veer left on SH2, but continue on along what becomes Maunganui Road. It is then a simple matter of following it about 4km (2½ miles) before you are at '**The Mount**'. The major landmark is Mount Maunganui itself, a conical rocky feature rising

to a height of 232m (760ft) above sea level. The Mount is of major historical significance, being one of the largest sites of early Maori settlement in New Zealand.

The well sign-posted **Visitor Information Centre** on Salisbury Avenue, left off Maunganui Road (Tel: 575 5099) can give you a guide to walking the Mount, and other useful information. Alternatively, drive to the Mount's base, park

Te Puke Kiwifruit Country

near the Domain camp grounds, and follow signs to the start of the tracks. Make sure you are on the **Summit Road Track**, and not simply walking around the base of the Mount. It takes about an hour to get to the top, but the view from the lookout is spectacular. After the walk, treat yourself to a swim in the **Hot Salt Pools** at the Mount's base (Tel: 577 7201, open daily 8am–10pm).

Have a picnic on the beach, at any one of the sheltered spots on the harbour side (drive along The Mall) or near Moturiki Island (Marine Parade). Buy food from any of the inexpensive tearooms along Mount Maunganui Road.

After lunch, head into Tauranga, driving back along Maunganui Road, cutting a sharp right along SH29 (Hewletts Road) to cross the harbour bridge. Turn left and aim for the city centre and find parking, and an information office along **The Strand**. Take a walk in the well-maintained gardens of **Herries Park**. At the north end of the gardens is an impressively carved ceremonial Maori canoe, **Te Awanui**, cut from a single kauri tree. Looking up **McLean Street** away from the harbour you might see a huge aspen tree which according to legend began life as a stake for tethering horses. Just beyond is the historic **Old Post Office**, built in 1904.

Near **McLean Street**, just off the Strand is a path that leads to **Monmouth Redoubt** where British troops were stationed during unrest in the 1860s. It is now a picturesque spot graced by large pohutukawa trees.

Go north of the Redoubt for the gardens and glasshouses of **Robbins Park** and **The Elms Mission**, or south back along The Strand and up **Devonport Road** for some shopping.

Afternoon tea can be had at **Le Cafe**, left heading up Devonport Road, with its views over the harbour. Alternatively, driving south 3km (2 miles) down Cameron Road will take you to 17th Avenue, and the **Tauranga Historic Village**. It contains a variety of period shops, working craftspeople and vintage transport rides over its 6-ha (14-acre) complex.

If you are in Tauranga for dinner go tex-mex at **East Coasters** (77 Devonport Road, Tel: 578 9928, open Tuesday–Saturday from 6pm). **Harbourside** (Strand Extension, Tel: 571 0520, open daily from 11am) offers Mediterranean-style cuisine.

Allow yourself about 1½ hours for the return journey to Rotorua. Head back a short distance from the Historic Village and turn right, or south from the centre of the city and turn left, into 15th Avenue (SH2). From there just follow the signs to Te Puke, back to SH33 and home.

Wellington

DAY ①

Victoria Street to Queen's Wharf

This walking tour takes you up by cable car for a view over the capital city. Walk through the Botanic Gardens and have morning tea at the Botanic Gardens Cafe. A stroll through the historic Bolton Street Memorial Park takes you to the Beehive and Parliament Building. Lunch at the Backbencher pub, and return to the city via the waterfront and the Maritime Museum.

It seems ironic to many that New Zealand's erstwhile 'movers and shakers' – the politicians – should be based on a piece of real estate itself so prone to moving and shaking – Wellington. But the twin

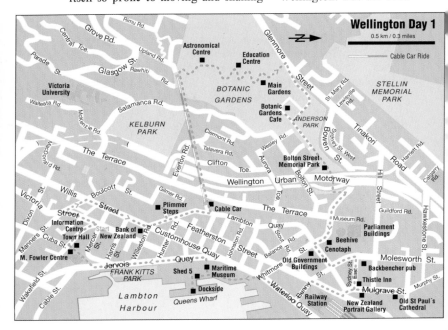

Wellington Day 1
0.5 km / 0.3 miles

Cable Car Ride

forces of politics and nature combine to make the city and the region surrounding it, a place of unique charm.

The itinerary begins at the **City Information Centre** (corner of Victoria and Wakefield streets, Tel: 801 4000, open daily 8.30am–5.30pm, extended hours in summer). Find a convenient carpark just beside the Plaza International Hotel on Wakefield Street and gather maps and information on local events. Walk the short distance along Victoria Street, following the flow of traffic, to **Manners Street**.

This area can be regarded as the top end of Wellington's downtown with, to your left, Manners Mall leading to Cuba Mall and Courtenay Place. **Cuba Street**, which runs off Cuba Mall has developed considerably in recent years and now boasts some great cafes, and restaurants, albeit with a bohemian flavour. Remnants of its past seedy reputation are evident in the odd strip joint, but it is interesting to explore.

Turn right on Manners Street and walk to Willis Street where the interplay between commerce and the commercial becomes more intense. Heading north-east (a right turn from Manners Street) you will pass on your left the home of the capital's two daily papers – the *Dominion* and *The Evening Post*, a variety of shops, cafes and bars, and also banks and business headquarters. Watch out for the tall and distinctive black-panelled **Bank of New Zealand** building on the right side of the road. Escalators lead down to an extensive underground shopping precinct.

With the Bank of New Zealand building as a landmark, veer left away from it and up **Lambton Quay**. If you are wondering what a quay is doing when there is no water in the immediate vicinity, the answer is that things were very different 150 years ago. **Wakefield Street**, along Lambton Quay to Thorndon Quay, marks Wellington's old foreshore before an earthquake in the 1850s reclaimed some more land.

Stay on the left side of Lambton Quay because there is more to see, though mainly in the way of shopping. Watch

Lambton Quay

out for the **Plimmer Steps**, 80m (85yds) from the corner. Part way up the steps which lead to Boulcott Street is the peculiarly sited **Plimmer Oak**, which legend has it grew from an acorn given by Governor George Grey to John Plimmer (1812–1905), an early Wellington settler and businessman.

Our main target is a further 150m (85yds) along Lambton Quay – the **Wellington Cable Car** (Monday to Friday 7am–10pm, Sat-

Wellington Cable Car ride

urday 9.20am–6pm, and Sunday 10.30am–6pm). The cars leave regularly every 10 minutes or so from Lambton Quay and take you effortlessly up a steep incline, under the motorway and over Kelburn Park, to Upland Road and a magnificent view back over the city and its harbour.

Get off and head for the adjacent **Botanic Gardens**. If the heavens interest you, take a look at the **Astronomical Centre** (Tel: 472 5053, open daily 9am–5pm) which has a planetarium and observatory. Walk around behind it and you will see the interesting **Sundial of Human Involvement** which commemorates the arrival of Plimmer in Wellington.

In the summer months, with the flowers in bloom, the gardens are particularly spectacular. But they are always peaceful and ideal for a quiet stroll. Wander off the main paths to fully appreciate the gardens, but ultimately aim for the **Education and Environment Centre** (Monday to Friday 9am–4pm, weekends and public holidays 10am–4pm), where you learn about New Zealand flora from a variety of interesting displays.

Lady Norwood Rose Garden

Follow the road down through the flower beds of the **Main Garden** to Glenmore Street. Turn right out of the large iron gates, but re-enter the park 50m (55yds) further down at the Centennial Entrance to the **Lady Norwood Rose Garden**, and then, Botanic Gardens Cafe for morning tea. The rose garden, which blooms from November through April, displays a huge variety of roses in a classical formal garden design.

Just behind is the **Begonia House** which comprises an indoor plant display, a tropical section and a Giant Water Lily House, and a cafe (open daily 9am–4pm). Its glasshouse style surroundings make you feel like you are supping in some exotic rainforest.

Follow the path past the top end of Anderson Park to the **Bolton Street Memorial Park** and through the old city cemetery where many famous New Zealanders have been laid to rest.

Turn left at the bottom of the cemetery, crossing the motorway via the overbridge. The path leads you by the **Wakefield Graves** where Edward Gibbon Wakefield (1796–1862), the man who organised the preliminary expedition to establish settlements in New Zealand, is buried.

Follow the path signposted to the Parliament Buildings and Lambton Quay which leads you down onto Bowen Street and very soon, a view of the **Beehive** on your left. The circular, copper-domed building houses the executive wing of Parliament, including

42

the office of the Prime Minister.

On your right you will pass **Alexander Turnbull House**, formerly owned by an early settler, Alexander Turnbull (1868–1918) who combined a liking for 'the bottle' with a passion for books, and who by the time of his death, had assembled one of the finest collections of historic writing on New Zealand and the Pacific area.

From the **Cenotaph** at the base of Bowen Street there are several things to do. The marble **Parliament Building**, built in 1922, has been undergoing major renovations and structural repairs, with Bowen House just across the road standing in as a temporary base. Across the road from the Cenotaph back on Lambton Quay is the old **Government Buildings**, built in 1876 and constructed entirely of wood. The structure, using more than 9,290sq m (100,000sq ft) of timber, is the largest wooden building in the southern hemisphere, and the second largest in the world (after a Japanese temple). The building is currently being renovated and refurbished for the Law Society and the Victoria University.

If you're hungry, turn left off Lambton Quay beyond the old Government Buildings and walk 200m (220yds) up Molesworth Street to the **Backbencher** pub and cafe. Billed as the 'house with no peers' the pub attracts more than the occasional politician, courtesy of its location opposite the Beehive, and is decorated with cartoons and caricatures of political figures from a popular satirical television programme.

Dropping down East Sydney Street 50m (55yds) to the Mulgrave Street corner is the **Thistle Inn**. It is not as inviting as the Backbencher pub, but interesting for being the oldest 'licensed establishment' on its original premises (circa 1840) in New Zealand.

Turning left up Mulgrave Street takes you past first the **National Archives**, and then the **New Zealand Portrait Gallery** (Tel: 495 6211, Monday to Friday 9am–5pm, admission free) which stages varied ex-

Backbencher pub

hibitions along Kiwi cultural themes. Another 100m (110yds) further on is **Old St Paul's Cathedral** (Tel: 473 6722, Monday to Saturday 10am–4.30pm). This beautiful historic Wellington church is a fine example of timbered Gothic construction.

From Old St Paul's Cathedral, retrace your steps back along Mulgrave Street. You have a walk of about a kilometre to the

Wellington harbourside

Wellington **Harbourside**. Cross Lambton Quay and follow Featherston Street. Turn left into Bunny Street past the Railway Station and then right into Waterloo Quay. Cross the road and enter any of the gates you find into the harbour area. It is open to the public, and though much of the area is given over to car-parking, it gets you off the busy road. About 500m (550yds) from the Railway station you will come to **Queen's Wharf**. There are two superb new developments on the wharf area.

Shed 5 Restaurant and Bar (Tel: 499 9069, open daily noon–3pm, 6–10.30pm; cafe open from 11am to late) dishes out some great New Zealand food. Next door is the moderately-priced **Dockside Restaurant and Bar** (Tel: 499 9900, open daily for lunch, dinner and Sunday brunch from 11am–11pm), imaginatively sited in a 100-year-old wharf building.

After a late lunch, head for the **Maritime Museum** just next to the Customhouse Quay entrance to Queen's Wharf (Tel: 472 8904, Monday to Friday 9.30am–4pm, weekends and public holidays 1–4.30pm, admission by donation). The museum houses a captivating collection of maritime memorabilia.

Options after the museum include walking a couple of blocks west back into the central city area for some late afternoon shopping, or turning left down Jervois Quay, walking along the new harbourside developments, including **Frank Kitts Park**, to the **Michael Fowler Centre**, named after a recent long-serving mayor of Wellington. The centre and the elegant Edwardian **Wellington Town Hall** together host a wide range of cultural events and is also the venue for the biennial New Zealand International Festival of the Arts.

Crossing Jervois Quay and walking through the twin facilities will lead you back to where the itinerary started – Wakefield Street and the City Information Centre. From here, either return to your hotel for a rest before checking out the city's nightlife options, or take the chance for a late afternoon drive around Oriental Parade and up Mount Victoria (see *Pick & Mix 5*).

Michael Fowler Centre

5. Evening Drive to Oriental Parade

A 1-hour driving excursion up to Mount Victoria lookout and around Oriental Parade returning via the Museum of New Zealand Te Papa Tongarewa.

To give you a glimpse of the capital's diversity, this itinerary can be tagged on as an evening drive to round off your day in Wellington. Alternatively, it can be extended by half an hour by simply following a circular route around Wellington's rugged eastern bays beyond the airport.

The first target is **Mount Victoria Lookout**, which can be reached from the eastern end of Courtenay Place. Cross both Cambridge Terrace and Kent Terrace before continuing east two blocks up Majoribanks Street. Follow the signs, turning left into Hawker Street, past the brick-red St Gerard's Monastery to the Lookout and you will be rewarded with a great view back over the city and the harbour. Return along the same route

View from Victoria Lookout

crossing over Kent Terrace to get to Cambridge Terrace where you turn right. Drive towards the harbour and through a rather confusing intersection, veering right into **Oriental Parade**. The drive takes you past the Port Nicholson Yacht Club and Freyberg Pool and Fitness Centre on your left.

Oriental Parade takes you past both some expensive Wellington real estate, and some fine Wellington restaurants. With its romantic views you may want to return here later for dinner. Walk the foreshore if you feel like it, or continue around past the White Lady Lighthouse, Balaena Bay and the Evans Bay Marina.

Oriental Parade offers an alternative route to the airport and the Eastern Bays by turning left around Evans Bay. To return to the city, turn right into Wellington Road and drive up to Ruahine Street, following signs to the Mount Victoria tunnel. The tunnel leads through the hill and down to what is effectively a large

45

Stroll along Oriental Parade

roundabout, with the centre being the Basin Reserve, an international cricket venue. Circling around 'The Basin', turn left into Buckle Street and just 200m (218yds) along is the entrance to the **Museum of New Zealand Te Papa Tongarewa** (Tel: 385 9609, open daily 9am–5pm). The museum houses some of New Zealand's major national treasures.

The city centre is easily reached by turning right off Buckle Street into Taranaki Street. It leads you back to Wakefield Street and the City Information Centre.

6. Kapiti Coast

This easy half-day itinerary takes you out of Wellington along SH1 through Paekakariki, Paraparaumu and Waikanae beaches on the Kapiti Coast. Highlights are the Lindale Farm Park, the Southward Car Museum, and coastal views of Kapiti Island.

The **Kapiti Coast** is a 40-km (25-mile) drive from Wellington but can take longer than you expect because of the volume of traffic. Parts of the route are frustrating bottlenecks at rush hour, so I would advise you to have a leisurely breakfast and push off after 9am. To escape the city, drive up the one-way Vivian Street and follow the signs to the Wellington/Hutt Motorway.

About 7km (4 miles) along, turn off to the left, following SH1 up the Ngauranga Gorge and through Johnsonville and Tawa. The highway bisects the beaches and boats of Porirua Harbour, and af-

Kapiti countryside

ter Plimmerton hugs the coast tightly as the Tararua range up to the right. Watch out for views of **Kapiti Island** to the north. Kapiti was the stronghold of the famous Maori chief, Te Rauparaha, who won the island in a battle in the 1820s. It was turned into a native forest and bird reserve at the turn of the century and is now one of the country's most valuable sanctuaries.

About 15km (9 miles) beyond Plimmerton, you come to **Paekakariki**, and just beyond that, at McKay's Crossing, Queen Elizabeth Park, is the **Wellington Tramway Museum** (Tel: 292 8361). Unfortunately, the museum is open only infrequently – on weekends and public holidays from 11am–5pm. If you are there at the right time, it is worth taking time out for a return tram ride to the beach.

Continuing on 11km (7 miles) you reach **Paraparaumu**. Watch for the Coastlands shopping development on your left and turn off if you can, because in the forecourt of the precinct is the **Kapiti Information Centre**. The staff there can give you advice on a whole range of activities if you want to spend more time in the area. Otherwise, continue on along the Main Road north and watch for the signs to the **Lindale Farm Park** (Tel: 297 0916, open daily 9am–5pm). This unique complex offers farm shows at 2pm every weekend, but at any time you can watch cheese being made, and walk around the Farm Park to feed the baby animals. Try the superb Kapiti ice cream at the restaurant or gift shop there.

Next, visit the **Southward Car Museum** (Tel: 297 1221, open daily 9am–4.30pm), which has one of the largest and most comprehensive privately owned collection of veteran and vintage cars in the Southern Hemisphere. Even if automobiles are not your scene, Southward will impress. You will see vehicles ranging from an 1895 Benz carriage to a 1981 stainless steel De Lorean.

Stop for lunch at **Country Life** (Tel: 293 6353, open Tuesday to Sunday), sited in a beautiful old villa right beside the main road beyond the Southward turn-off just before **Waikanae**.

Feel free to explore Waikanae as time allows. There are many craft studios in the area and also the **Nga Manu Sanctuary** (turn left just before the shopping centre and then right 3km (2 miles) down Ngarara Road) which offers pleasant walks through native bush.

On the way back to Wellington, take the alternative route offered by the **Paekakariki Hill Road** at Paekakariki. The historic road takes you through some bush-covered hills to a great lookout point and on to **Pauatahanui**. Turn left and the road links up with SH2 in the Hutt Valley. From there it is a simple 20-km (12½-mile) trip back into the city.

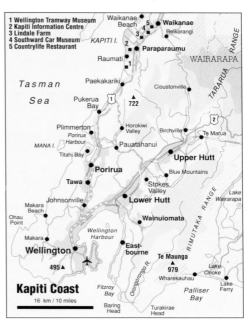

CHRISTCHURCH

DAY ①

Avon River to Mona Vale

Walk along the banks of the Avon River. Visit the centre of Christchurch, Cathedral Square, the Arts Centre and the Botanic Gardens. Walk to the Antigua Boat Sheds, and back into the centre of the city for some shopping in Cashel Mall. Then, either ride the Mount Cavendish Gondola or visit the stately Mona Vale.

Christchurch is an elegant city; English in style and grace, nestling up to the extinct volcanic landscape of the Port Hills. Sweeping away north, south and west are the expansive Canterbury Plains – flat, prairie-type farm lands that grew from the alluvial wash of the grand Southern Alps. East is the Pacific, which butts up to grey-sand beaches and has punctured old craters and valleys of Banks Peninsula to form a variety of natural harbours.

Begin this walking itinerary at the **Visitor Centre** opposite Noah's Hotel on the corner of Worcester Street and Oxford Terrace (Tel: 379 9629, Monday to Friday 8.30am–5pm, weekends and public holidays 8.30am–4pm, extended hours in summer). Convenient parking is available at the public carpark just next to Noah's.

A variety of activities are available from outside the Visitor Centre, including **punting** on the

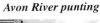
Avon River punting

Avon (open daily 9am–7pm in summer) and the unique **Vintage Car Tours** (Tel: 323 8132) that takes you in style around some of the city's highlights – an ideal option if you are pushed for time.

Follow the punting route on foot by walking north along Oxford Terrace to Gloucester Street.

48

The stately Canterbury Provincial Buildings

Turn left and cross the Gloucester Street Bridge, and you will find a path that leads along the Avon's west bank beside the **Canterbury Provincial Building** (Tel: 366 1100, guided tours available from Monday to Saturday 10.30am–2.30pm, closed Sunday). The buildings are the only remaining provincial government buildings in New Zealand and were built between 1859 and 1865. A 100-m (109yds) walk brings you out onto Armagh Street opposite the Law Courts, and if you cross back over the river you will arrive at **Victoria Square**.

Wander around the square at your leisure, perhaps trying a vanilla ice-cream from the mobile stand on Armargh Street. Victoria Square is a popular venue amongst staff of nearby offices for outdoor summer lunches when bands play in the amphitheatre in front of the Parkroyal Hotel. At Christmas time, the entire square

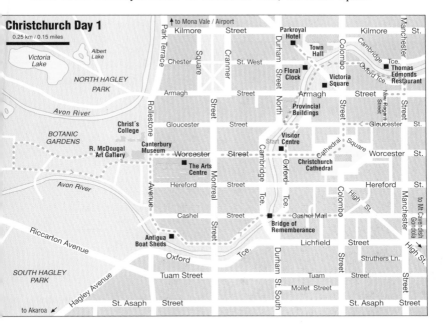

is filled with people for the traditional singing of 'Carols by Candlelight'.

Statues of Queen Victoria and Captain Cook grace the square in front of **Hamish Hay Bridge**, reputedly the first cast-iron and stone bridge of its type in New Zealand when it was built in 1863.

Beyond the bridge to the left of the amphitheatre is the **Floral Clock**, a feature of this 'Garden City' for many decades, while to the right of the Parkroyal is the **Christchurch Town Hall**, the city's main concert and convention venue.

The **Victoria Street Cafe** on the entrance level of the **Parkroyal Hotel** is a perfect place for a meal. Or else, go next door to the Town Hall and ask for a table overlooking the Avon River.

Leave Victoria Square by crossing the north-south running Colombo Street and follow Oxford Terrace as it resumes winding its way along the banks of the Avon River. On your left you will see the beautifully restored **Thomas Edmonds Restaurant**, converted from a band rotunda, and the site of another punting operation on the river. Ahead, a strand of poplar trees line the Avon River, making for a particularly beautiful scene when draped in their autumn colours.

Turn right into Manchester Street and in the distance you should see the Port Hills. Turn right again into Armagh Street where the first left brings you to **New Regent Street** with its charming Edwardian facades painted in pastel blues and yellows.

Turn right into Gloucester Street past the Theatre Royal and then first left into Colombo Street and you are at the geographic centre of Christchurch, **Cathedral Square**. The pedestrian only area attracts a wide cross-section of Christchurch society, from local executives to hip teenagers. Like Victoria Square, it is a busy lunch-time venue and often features council-run activities in the summer. An interesting character you may see around (he 'disappears' from June to mid-August) is **The Wizard of Christchurch** who takes to a soap-box at lunchtime and holds forth on a variety of topics. Do not treat him lightly as he has been granted the status of 'A Living Work of Art'.

Prime position in the square is held by the grey-stoned **Christchurch Cathedral**, with its 63-m (208-ft)

The imposing Christchurch Cathedral

tower. Visitors can climb to look-out balconies via a spiral staircase of 133 steps for panoramic views of the city (open daily 8.30am–6pm). There are also free guided tours of the Cathedral given at 11am and 2pm Monday to Friday, 11am on Saturday and 11.30am on Sunday.

Around the perimeter of Cathedral Square are duty-free shopping outlets and the offices of the South Island's largest daily newspaper, *The Press*.

Leave Cathedral Square by heading past the statue of John Robert Godley, the city's founder, and west along Worcester Street. Cross the river by the Information Centre and head two blocks further west until you reach the **Arts Centre**.

The neo-Gothic stone buildings formerly housed Canterbury University, but now is a focal point for artists and craftspeople. Attractions include the **Court Theatre**, **Southern Ballet Theatre**, the **Academy Cinema** and the **Great Hall**. There are a wide variety of craft studios within the complex, so browse around. Check out the **Christchurch Bone Carving Studio** and the **Riki Rangi Maori Carving Studio** for tradi-

tional Maori crafts. This whole area comes alive on weekends with a market from 10am–4pm (and also Fridays in the summer). Sample some of the offerings from the exotic food stalls.

At the end of Worcester Street across the Arts Centre is the **Canterbury Museum** (Tel: 366 8379, open daily 9am–4.30pm, admission by donation) which houses a variety of permanent displays,

Weekend market at the Arts Centre

including the world class Edgar Stead Hall of New Zealand Birds and the Hall of Antarctic Discovery. A recently opened gallery focusing on the extinct moa, New Zealand's most famous pre-historic bird, is also worth a look. Free guided tours of the museum are held at 10.15am, 11.30am, 1.15am and 2.30pm daily.

North of the museum are the grounds of the private boys' school, **Christ's College**, while south and west are the extensive **Botanic Gardens**. Established in 1863, the gardens are a remarkable transformation given the fact that the land was once covered in tussock and bracken.

Take a leisurely stroll through the gardens to the tea kiosk. A battery-powered tour vehicle takes visitors on guided tours daily, leaving from outside the Information Centre. The smorgasbord lunch at the tea kiosk is also worth a try.

The **Robert McDougal Art Gallery**, adjacent to the museum and within the Botanic Gardens, has an impressive permanent collection of paintings, and has regular special exhibits (Tel: 365 0914, open daily 10am–4.30pm, admission free).

Leave the Botanic Gardens via Rolleston Avenue (the way you went in) and turn right to join up with the Avon again. If you are feeling adventurous, try a popular Christchurch family pastime – boating on the Avon – with paddle boats and canoes available for hire from the **Antigua Boat Sheds**. Alternatively, buy an ice-cream from the Boat Shed Snack Bar and continue along the river.

About 200m (218yds) across Montreal Street and around the river, the road joins **Cashel Street**, a pedestrian area lined with shops. To your right is the distinctive archway of the **Bridge of Remembrance**, a World War I memorial, and beyond that, **Cashel Mall**, a pedestrian area lined with shops. End this part of the tour by browsing along the Mall. To return to the Visitor Centre, walk two blocks north on Oxford Terrace following the river.

To round off your day in Christchurch, take an afternoon excursion out of the city centre. Top of the list of options is a ride up the Port Hills on the **Mount Cavendish Gondola** (Tel: 384 4914, open daily 10am until late). The Gondola takes you on a 367-m (400-yds) vertical rise ride to the rim of the long extinct Lyttelton Volcano. From the viewing gallery you get a panorama of Christchurch, over to Lyttelton Harbour, out to the Pacific and over the Canterbury Plains to the Southern Alps. To get there, a free shuttle bus service, the Gondola Bus, leaves at regular intervals from the city centre. Check at the Visitor Centre. If you are driving yourself, follow Ferry Road, which runs off Moorhouse Avenue south-east and take the Tunnel Road turn-off.

Alternatively, just 1¾km (1 mile) from the centre of Christchurch is the charm and grace of the elegant **Mona Vale** homestead (63 Fendalton Road, Tel: 348 9660, April to September daily 8.30am–5pm, October to March daily 8am–7.30pm).

The Elizabethan-style mansion was built in 1905 and a scrumptious Devonshire cream tea is served amidst the wonderful setting. Walk the gardens, have a late afternoon picnic, feed the ducks, or indulge yourself with a romantic punt ride. To get to Mona Vale,

follow the route out of the city to the airport (left at the north end of Hagley Park along Harper Avenue) and make a right turn into Fendalton Road. Mona Vale is located just before the railway line. If you're not driving to Mona Vale, catch the No. 9 bus from the city centre.

Elegant Mona Vale

7. Hanmer Springs

This full day itinerary takes you north of Christchurch on SH1, through rich farmland of the Canterbury Plains. Turn inland along SH7, and onto route 7A, to the hot springs resort of Hanmer. Climb Conical Hill, walk the forests and have a refreshing soak in the thermal pools before embarking on the return journey to Christchurch.

Hanmer Springs, nestled amongst foothills of the Southern Alps, is the South Island's main thermal resort. Surrounded by vast tracts of indigenous and native forests in a landscape cut by sometimes meandering and at other times roaring rivers, a day trip to Hanmer Springs combines scenic beauty with plenty to do.

Hanmer is 135km (84 miles) from Christchurch, with the drive taking about two hours. An easy route out of the city is to get onto Victoria Street heading away from the Parkroyal Hotel and continuing straight along, veering right at the end of Papanui Road, out onto the motorway and SH1.

Along the route you will cross wide shingle river-beds that drain from the Southern Alps. Though the water levels are often low in summer, flash floods in the Alps can cause the water to rise rapidly and extensive stop banks have been built to help prevent flooding.

Waipara Junction and the turn-off to SH7 (signposted to Arthur's Pass) signals the half-way point in the journey and makes a good place to stop to stretch your legs. Have tea at the **Waipara Tea Junction** (Tel: 314 6769) with its large sign welcoming you to 'Moa Country'. Apparently, the giant, but now extinct moa used to roam these plains hundreds of years ago.

Driving on you will come to the birch-lined **Weka Pass** (named after a cheeky native New Zealand bird). Look out for strange rocky outcrops such as **Frog Rock**.

Between Waikari and Culverden is the historic **Hurunui Hotel**, with its peaceful garden bar and traditional pub atmosphere. The Hurunui holds the longest continuous license of any pub in the

South Island, having been in operation since 1860 and the publican, Robin Denley, is guaranteed to make you feel welcome if you call in now or on your way back.

About 110km (68 miles) from Christchurch is the SH7A Hanmer turn-off. Make the turn, but watch for the carpark 200m (219yds) ahead on your right. Turn into the carpark for dramatic views of 'Thrillseekers' Canyon'. A short walk to the Waiau Ferry Bridge will show you how the gorge got its name. Bungy jumpers leap from the bridge, and down in the fast-flowing Waiau River, spectacular jet boat rides are offered. Enjoy the view or join in the activities, then continue on to Hanmer, another 25km (15½ miles) up the road.

The **Hurunui Visitor Information Centre** (open weekdays 9am–5pm, weekends 9.45am–5pm), run by the Department of Conservation, is adjacent to the hotpools, on the left as you enter the town. It can provide you with lots of information, including details of some wonderful bush walks through meadowlands and various stands of exotic timber. One walk you must do is up the zig-zag track on **Conical Hill**, just behind the town. The lookout at the top offers magnificent views over the Hanmer Basin.

For lunch, try the **Alpine Village Inn** (Jacks Pass Road, Tel: 315 7085) just behind the shopping centre, or home-cooked cafe food at the friendly **Village Plus Cafe** on Conical Hill Road.

The **Hanmer Springs Thermal Reserve** (Tel: 315 7511, open daily 10am–8pm) is obviously the central attraction of the town and offers a variety of top-class facilities, including three thermal pools, private pools and a freshwater pool. It is ideal for an afternoon of relaxation after Conical Hill or other bush walks, or perhaps a round of golf at the charming Hanmer Springs Country Club. Hanmer is a good all-season venue, with nearby skiing offered at the **Amuri Ski-field**.

Hanmer Springs hotpools

If you are still soaking away the time in the early evening, you may want to have dinner before returning to Christchurch. Try the **Old Post Office Restaurant** (Tel: 315 7461, open from 6pm in winter and 6.30pm in summer), just into Jacks Pass Road at the top end of town. Alternatively, renew your acquaintance with Robin at the Hurunui pub on your way home. It generally fills with local farmers or raucous skiers in the evening, depending on the time of year. Either way, it is a nice way to round off your day.

8. Akaroa

Follow SH75 out of Christchurch and around the base of the Banks Peninsula to the French-settled town of Akaroa. Walk the quaint streets and visit craft shops. Take a harbour cruise on the Canterbury Cat. Lunch at the French Farm Winery on the opposite shore before returning to Christchurch at mid-afternoon.

Akaroa, just 84km (52 miles) from Christchurch, holds a unique place for many in the history of New Zealand. But aside from that it is simply a wonderful place to visit, and easily reached by car from Christchurch.

Verdant Banks Peninsula

Leave Christchurch along Hagley Avenue on the southern boundary of Hagley Park and follow straight out Lincoln Road. SH75 takes you through the townships of Halswell and Taitapu and around Banks Peninsula.

South of Motukarara, the road will pass alongside Lake Ellesmere, a large coastal lagoon, before turning sharply left and following beside the picturesque Lake Forsyth. Just beyond the head of the lake is the settlement of **Little River** where you can stop and look at the crafts on display in the old railway building.

Continuing on, the road climbs steeply out of Cooptown and up to the appropriately named **Hilltop**. Drive in to the carpark by the

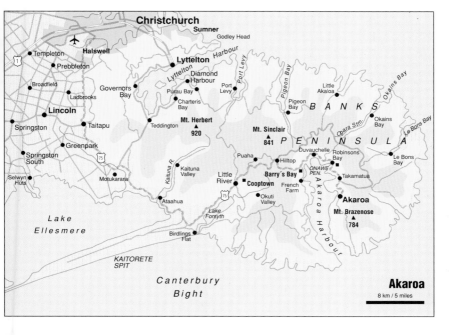

Akaroa

8 km / 5 miles

Hilltop Tavern for a grand view out over the **Onawe Peninsula** and **Akaroa Harbour**. The peninsula was the site of a Maori *pa* (fortified village), constructed in 1831 by the Ngai Tahu to meet a threat of invasion from a northern Maori tribe. Drive down past Barry's Bay, Duvauchelle and Takamatua to **Akaroa**.

The town has a fascinating history, evidenced by the French road signs as you drive in. In 1838, Jean Langlois, the captain of a French whaling ship, negotiated the purchase of Banks Peninsula from a local Maori chief. On his return to France he organised a group of emigrants who sailed for Akaroa. They arrived in the Bay of Islands only to hear that the Treaty of Waitangi had been signed and British sovereignty over New Zealand declared. The emigrants decided to continue on to Akaroa and settle anyway. In 1849, Langlois's settlement company sold its assets and land claims to the New Zealand Company. In 1850, the French settlers were joined by a larger group of British colonists.

Akaroa War Memorial

The French influence has remained strong and can best be experienced by walking around the charming streets at the northern end of the town. Find a parking space just as you enter Akaroa and walk along **Rue Lavaud**. Visit **Langlois-Eteveneaux Cottage** and the **Akaroa Museum** (Tel: 304 7614, open daily 10.30am –4.30pm in summer, 10.30am–4pm in winter) on the corner of Rue Lavaud and Rue Balgueri. The cottage, prefabricated in France, is one of the oldest in Canterbury. Behind the cottage, the museum has a variety of interesting displays.

Also on Rue Balgueri is **St Patrick's Church**, built in 1863. Walk up Rue Balgueri to **Settlers Hill** and a track takes you to **L'Aube Hill Reserve** and the **Old French Cemetery**, the first consecrated burial ground in Canterbury. Walk back to Rue Lavaud and enjoy a stroll south beside the gardens, with its centrepiece **War Memorial**, to the sweeping beachside promenade. On a nice day you can easily walk the mile around the bay to the English part of town, taking in the views across the inlet. Otherwise, drive the same route and look for a park near the Akaroa pier, a popular place for fishing. Join up for a cruise on the **Canterbury Cat** that plies the harbour at 11am and 1.30pm (Tel: 304 7641). It is a great 2-hour trip to the headlands, and if you are visiting in summer you may glimpse rare Hectors dolphins en route.

If you return hungry, there are plenty of eating places, including the **Pier Cafe** on the wharf itself and, along Beach Road, the trendy **Astrolabe** for pizza and French pastries. If it is summer and you want a real treat however, circle back around the harbour, carry on past Barry's Bay and along the low road to the **French Farm Winery** (Tel: 304 5784, open daily 10am–6pm) for an inexpensive meal, complemented with local wine in a sheltered garden setting. Return via the Hilltop to Christchurch.

9. Mount Cook and the Glaciers

No trip to New Zealand would be complete without a visit to the spectacular glaciers. This option is perfect as a stopover on the flight (or drive) from Christchurch to Queenstown.

If you are flying from Christchurch to Queenstown, a spectacular diversion is offered en route by the glaciers and mountains of the **Southern Alps**. Mount Cook Airlines has flights which offer stopover options at **Mount Cook Village**, near **Mount Cook** itself – New Zealand's highest mountain (3,764m/12,348ft). From the small airport in the Hooker Valley, transfer to a skiplane flight in the midst of some of the most awe-inspiring scenery anywhere in the world.

Taking in the Southern Alps

The magnificent Grant Circle option lasts for about 1¼ hours and flies you to the West Coast of the main divide. You will first view, and then land on either the **Franz Joseph** or **Fox Glaciers**, and then step out onto these spectacular ice flows. There is the thrill of the take-off on ice, and more stunning scenery as you cross the divide again and swoop over the

Tasman Glacier, the longest temperate glacier in the world. Alternative trips include the Glacier Highlights, or Ski the Tasman tours if you decide to extend your stay here.

Have lunch, or morning or afternoon tea at the unique **Hermitage** (Tel: 435 1809). A famous tourist hotel situated up the Hooker Valley, the Hermitage can be reached by bus from the small Mount Cook Airport. Surrounded by majestic mountains, the hotel is also an ideal stop-over destination if you are driving to Queenstown and want to break up the journey (turn-off the main highway and follow the signs alongside Lake Pukaki). A wide range of hotel and chalet rooms are available, varying from mid-range to expensive.

Tasman Glacier

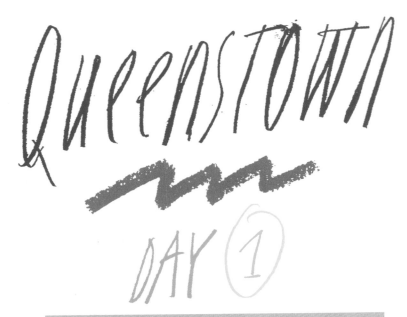

QUEENSTOWN

DAY ①

Skyline Gondola to Queenstown Bay

Have breakfast downtown and stroll along the streets before ascending the Skyline Gondola for a panoramic view of Lake Wakatipu and Queenstown. Head down and walk along the waterfront, perhaps signing up for a jet-boat ride on the Shotover or Kawarau rivers. Have lunch and then join the TSS Earnslaw on an afternoon excursion to Walter Peak, capping the day off with a late afternoon stroll around the Queenstown Gardens.

Resting on the shore of Lake Wakatipu, with high peaked mountains looming all around and valleys cut deep by swift-flowing rivers, Queenstown, in central Otago, is the quintessential year-round holiday resort. The town itself mixes the charm of its history and the grandeur of its natural setting with a dash of brashness that accompanies most resorts of its kind. The result is that day or night, there is always something to do there.

Because of its relatively small size, Queenstown is easy to get to know. With its extensive lake frontage to the south and south-west, the hills surrounding the town, and the streets following a grid pattern, it is very difficult to get lost. Start your day with a strong cuppa at **The Naff Caff** (62 Shotover Street, Tel: 442 8211).

When you are charged up and ready to go, head for the **Intercity Visitor Information Centre** in the Clocktower Centre on the corner of Shotover Street and Camp Street (Tel: 442 4100, open daily from 7am). Pick up maps and get advice on the huge range of activities on offer in this exciting town, and then begin your walking itinerary.

Cross Shotover Street and walk two blocks north-west up Camp Street. Turn left into Isle Street, past the fire station and then first right into Brecon Street. This takes you to your first destination, the **Skyline Gondola** (Tel: 442 7860, open daily from 10am).

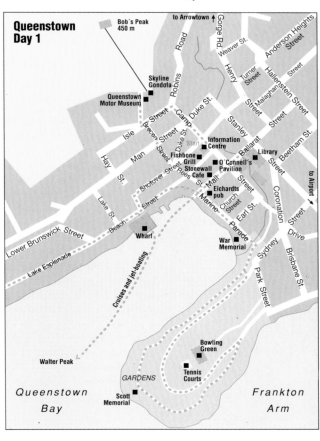

View of Lake Wakatipu and the Remarkables

The gondola goes on a vertical rise of 450m (490yds) up Bob's Peak to a magnificent view of Queenstown, **Lake Wakatipu** and **The Remarkables** mountain range. Alternatively, if it is a nice day, you could follow the track up to the top (it is steep, but straightforward: allow about 30 minutes up – and a lot less down!). There are walking tracks from the top, a restaurant, a gift shop and an outdoor viewing deck. Sign up for a dose of *Kiwi Magic* – a 30-minute movie showcasing the scenic splendour of New Zealand. This is not your usual travelogue but an exhilarating piece of cinema that will give you ideas on how to spend the rest of your time in New Zealand (on the hour every hour from 11am–9pm daily).

Coming down from the Gondola on Brecon Street, you will find another activity that may tempt you: the **Queenstown Motor Museum** (tel: 442-8775). Otherwise, wander down Brecon Street, turn right at Shotover Street and follow the road around to the Queenstown wharf area. The wharf is home to a variety of vessels, but none so distinctive as the TSS **Earnslaw**, affectionately known to locals as 'The Lady of the Lake'. The *Earnslaw* was built in sections

**Queenstown
Day 1**

Bob's Peak
450 m

to Arrowtown

Gorge Rd.
Weaver St.
Anderson Heights Street
Turner Street
Hallenstein Street

Road
Robins
Henry Street
Skyline Gondola
Queenstown Motor Museum
Camp Street
Duke St.
Brecon Street
Isle
Duke St.
Stanley Street
Malaghan Street
Beetham St.
Man St.
Hay St.
Information Centre
Ballarat Street
Library
Fishbone Grill
Stonewall Cafe
O'Connell's Pavilion
Shotover Street
Rees St.
Mall St.
Eichardts pub
Coronation Drive
to Airport
Lake St.
Marine Parade
Church Street
Earl St.
Lower Brunswick Street
Beach Street
Lake Esplanade
Wharf
War Memorial
Sydney Street
Brisbane St.
Cruises and jet-boating
Park Street
Bowling Green
Walter Peak
Tennis Courts
GARDENS
Queenstown
Bay
Scott Memorial
Frankton
Arm

*TSS **Earnslaw** with The Remarkables in the background*

in Dunedin, transported by rail to Kingston at the southern reach of Lake Wakatipu, reassembled and launched in February 1912. She is the last of many steamers that plied the waters of the lake in service of the farms on the lake's shores.

The coal-fired boilers belch out the *Earnslaw*'s trademark black smoke as she carries passengers on sightseeing tours. Go to the **Steamer Wharf** and book tickets (Tel: 442 7500) for the afternoon excursion to **Walter Peak** (leaves 2pm daily, more details later).

In the meantime, take a stroll away from town along **Lake Esplanade** to opposite the Youth Hostel for good views over the lake.

Alternatively, take the chance for a thrilling jet-boat ride. **Shotover Jets** (Tel: 442 8570) operate on the famous Shotover River. A courtesy bus departs from the station opposite the Visitor Information Centre on Shotover Street, taking the adventurous out to the jetty near **Arthur's Point** at regular intervals. The jet-boat drivers are top class and their sense of humour can be gauged by the smiles on their faces as they take you to within inches of overhanging

rocks! If you settle on this option, have lunch at **Cavell's Garden Bar and Restaurant** at Arthur's Point which overlooks the jet-boating antics from a spectacular perch. Other jet-boat rides leave right from the jetty or the wharf at **Queenstown Bay** and drive you wild for about an hour over a route around Frankton Arm, blasting through the Kawarau Dam and past the convergence with the Shotover. **Pro Jet** (Tel: 442 3034) and **Kawarau Jets** (Tel: 442 6142) are two of the main operators offering such tours.

On your return you may feel like get-

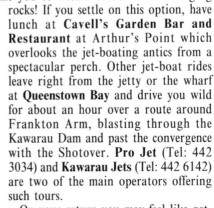

Shotover River

ting your 'land-legs' back by wandering around the **waterfront** and **The Mall** area, perhaps doing a little shopping. Though much of Queenstown has been taken over by modern tourist development, its charm is maintained by some of the century-old buildings, including the old pub of **Eichardts** (in operation since 1871) on Marine Parade and the courthouse and library buildings at the corner of Ballarat and Stanley Streets, built in 1876.

For lunch, try the food hall in **O'Connell's Pavilion** on Camp Street and Beach Street; for good seafood try the **Fishbone Grill** (Tel: 442 7309) opposite O'Connell's, while the **Stonewall Cafe** (Tel: 444 6429) along The Mall char-grills just about anything you want to perfection.

As 2pm draws near, make your way back to the wharf for your 3-hour *Earnslaw* cruise to **Walter Peak**. Situated on the western shore of the lake, Walter Peak is the original homestead of one of New Zealand's most famous sheep and cattle stations. The cruise across takes about 40 minutes and you have plenty of time to enjoy the beautiful gardens which surround the homestead. Included as part of the cruise is a traditional country-style afternoon tea with warm scones, fresh clotted cream and jam at **The Colonel's Homestead**. Then you're off to watch a sheep-shearing demonstration and inspect the unique herd of Scottish Highland cattle.

On board the Earnslaw to Walter Peak

Return to Queenstown and round the day off with a late afternoon stroll around the gardens on the other side of **Queenstown Bay**. Walk around past the jetty and along Marine Parade to the War Memorial. Follow the tree-lined promenade just behind the beach front and take the path at the end into the gardens. Initially, follow the paved road up and turn right, wandering alongside the pond past the bowling green and the tennis courts. Circle around the gardens at the lower end of the peninsula, and wander among the roses and the stones, watching for the dramatic memorial to Antarctic explorer Robert Falcon Scott.

Circling back on the east side of the tennis courts you come to a rollerskating rink; use that as the landmark to drop down to the lower tracks that circle around amongst the fir trees at shore level. Return by following this route around the bottom of the gardens and you will be rewarded with views first over the Frankton Arm to Kelvin Heights, then out over the middle reach of Lake Wakatipu towards Walter Peak, and finally back across Queenstown Bay to Queenstown itself.

Return along the beach-front to town.

10. Arrowtown

A half-day driving itinerary past the Shotover Gorge, Arthur's Point and up to Coronet Peak for a panoramic view of the Wakatipu Basin. Back down and around to Arrowtown, visiting the Colonial Museum and old miners' huts. Return via Lake Hayes and the Kawarau Bridge bungy jump operation.

A trip to **Arrowtown**, 21km (13 miles) from Queenstown, is a journey into the past. Nestled in a quiet gully, the town played a prominent role in the gold rush days of the 1860s, but as the gold diminished so did Arrowtown's importance. It did not, however, go the way of desolation like so many other gold mining settlements in the vicinity. Instead, it just slipped back into a quieter style of life, revelling in its beautiful location.

To get to Arrowtown from Queenstown, turn left off the north end of Shotover Street into Gorge Road. It is a spectacular route, lined with poplar trees that are especially stunning during autumn. About 6km (4 miles) out of Queenstown you pass **Arthur's Point Pub**, worth an excursion on its own for its traditional pub food, beer and atmosphere. About 500m (547yds) down you come to the historic **Edith Cavell bridge** spanning the scenic Shotover River.

Turn left at the end of the bridge and into the entrance to the **Shotover Jet-Boat** operation mentioned in the *Day 1 Queenstown* itinerary. If you haven't had the thrill of jetboating, then perhaps you may be tempted now. If not, at least watch the boats and hear the screams as travellers are whisked under the bridge and through the spectacular Shotover Gorge. A good spot to watch from is **Cavell's Garden Bar and Restaurant** where you can contemplate the challenge over a cup of tea, coffee, or something stronger.

Continue along what is now Malaghan Road; you will pass Arthur's Point Camp Ground on your right and the **Shotover Stables**, offering horse treks, on your left. Slow down as you pass **Nugget Point**, the superbly located lodge overlooking the Shotover River, because just beyond is the turn-off left to Coronet Peak

Jet-boating thrills

and Skippers Canyon. While Skippers Canyon is off-limits to most rental cars, **Coronet Peak** is not. In winter it is a top class ski-field with a fully sealed access road, and at all other times of year it is a superb lookout point from which to view the Wakatipu Basin. The drive up to the peak and back is about 20km (12 miles).

Return to Malaghan Road, turn left and resume your journey to Arrowtown. If you are interested in art, make a stop along Dalefield Road about 1km (½ mile) past the Coronet Peak turnoff, where you will find several galleries and woodturner Jim Robbie.

As you drive on, watch out for the **Millbrook Golf and Country Club** (Tel: 442 1563), a new development combining resort style accommodation and an 18-hole golf course designed by New Zealand's greatest golfer, left-hander Bob Charles. Just beyond Millbrook, turn left down Berkshire Street and you are in **Arrowtown**. Veer left along Berkshire Street and park in the Marshall Carpark on the corner of Berkshire Street and Buckingham Street, Arrowtown's main road.

Stroll down **Buckingham Street**. It feels like the set of some Hollywood movie, only a lot more authentic. There are

Arrowtown architecture and gold nuggets

craft and souvenir shops to browse around and also a number of historic landmarks – testimony to the small town's rich history. On the left, you will pass a monument to the Chinese goldminers who played an important role in the development of the region.

For shopping, try the **Arrow Emporium** (9–23 Buckingham Street). Indulge in an ice cream from the small shed next to Buckingham Green on your right. If you are after gold souvenirs, try **The Gold Shop** which sells crafted jewellery as well as nuggets at good prices. Just beyond The Gold Shop at **Athenaeum Hall** is a map and information board about Arrowtown, recounting some of the region's history, but for a more 'hands on' historical experience, go to the **Lakes District Centennial Museum** (open daily 9am–3pm) just before the corner with Wiltshire Street.

After your history lesson, cross the road to **The Stone Cottage** (Tel: 442 1860) for a heart-warming New Zealand country-style lunch in a historic stone house over a century old.

Just across the road from the Stone Cottage, in The Avenue of Old English Trees (the willow and sycamore-lined end of Buckingham Street), is Arrowtown's library, and behind that, further back is the old schist-built **Masonic Lodge**.

If you are feeling lucky, a great way to spend a half hour or so is to hire a gold pan from the friendly staff at **Hamilton's Grocery Store** back at the west end of Buckingham Street and try your hand at panning. Just go down to the river beyond the picnic area a block north of the main road and you meet the **Arrow River**. There is a fair chance you will garner a flake or two for your troubles.

To get a further insight into the hardships of mining a century ago, drive or walk to the **Arrowtown Chinese Camp**, 100m (109yds) west of the Marshall carpark. Walk between the plum and berry trees to the huts built into the hillside. Look for **Ah-Lums Store** on the left at the start of the small track and you might laugh at the Historic Places classification given to what looks like an old toilet. Note the lack of a door, but be amazed at the great views over Arrowtown from the facility.

Leaping off Kawarau Bridge

There are several routes out of Arrowtown, but I suggest driving back along Berkshire, and instead of turning into Malaghan Road, continue on for a scenic drive past Lake Hayes.

There are three diversions en route; a visit to **Waterfall Park**; a drive down **Speargrass Flat Road** to several artists' galleries, including Thomas L Brown's, and a winery; or a peep into **Walnut Cottage** (Tel: 442 1859, Tuesday to Sunday 9am–6pm, admission free). The cottage is over 120 years old and owned by a delightful couple who sell crafts, dried flowers and preserves.

Turn left at the bottom of Lake Hayes, following SH6 about 10km (6 miles) until you reach **Kawarau Bridge**, site of A J Hackett's bungy-jumping operation (Tel: 442 7100). Join in if you dare, but it is equally fascinating to watch others take the 43-m (47-yd) plunge off the historic bridge with just a glorified rubber band to halt their fall. This site is one of the first commercial bungy-jump operations in the world, fanning the craze that has swept the globe today. Return to Queenstown back along SH6.

11. Milford Sound

As a day trip you can coach or fly in to the spectacular natural glory of Milford Sound in Fiordland National Park. Cruise on the fiord and return by bus via the Homer Tunnel and Te Anau to Queenstown. Alternatively, with a return scenic air flight and cruise you can see Milford Sound in half a day.

Milford Sound is an unspoilt wonderland in the rainforest area of

New Zealand's deep south. Formed from a sunken glacial valley, Milford Sound (actually a fiord) is surrounded by steep bush-clad cliffs rising to the rugged mountains of the Southern Alps. It is the spectacular final destination of the world famous Milford Track, but you can reach it easily from Queenstown in a day.

Mount Cook Airline (Tel: 442 7650) flies to Milford five times daily in summer, and twice daily in winter, linking you with a spectacular **Red Boat** cruise around the sights of the Sound and returning you to Queenstown. Allow about 4 hours for this option.

Fairy Falls at Milford Sound

The **Milford Explorer** (Tel: 442 7650) coach departs Queenstown daily at 8am, driving you along one of the world's most beautiful scenic routes via Te Anau to Milford Sound for the spectacular Red Boat cruise. You can then return with Mount Cook Airline at 3.50pm. A cheaper option is to retrace your journey by coach arriving in Queenstown at 7.55pm. This is a very tiring, though still a worthwhile option.

Avoid driving yourself there and back in a day. Though it is possible to accomplish, the driving is difficult (with all the buses on the road), tiring (allow 4 to 5 hours each way), and you risk missing many of the sights along the way (while you are concentrating on not going over any cliffs!).

Whichever way you do make it to Milford Sound, bring your camera for some magnificent photo opportunities. You will see cascading waterfalls (successfully fill a cup of water from beneath **Fairy Falls** and you earn a dram of whisky from the Red Boat captain!), the fabulous form of **Mitre Peak** rising almost vertically from the sea floor, rare southern fur seals and possibly cruise along with dolphins. If you are there around Christmas-time watch also for the beautiful flowering Southern Rata, also known as the South Island Christmas Tree.

On the side of some of the sheer cliffs you will see veins of green, indicating traces of mineral deposits in the mountains. The Maori discovered this and were early visitors to the fiords in search of sacred greenstone.

Bring a waterproof jacket with you because Fiordland boasts the highest rainfall levels in the country. It seldom dampens the experience, but sandflies can. They thrive in the dampness of the region and though not harmful, their bites are extremely annoying. Covering up and dousing yourself liberally with insect repellent helps.

Photogenic fur seals

Shopping

For some people, shopping is the whole purpose of travel, while for others it is a necessary evil. Wherever you fit in the spectrum, shopping in New Zealand can be both enjoyable and enlightening. It can provide the impetus for getting out and about and mixing with the locals, or it can be a means of introduction to aspects of Kiwi history and culture.

New Zealand offers a wide range of shopping options, ranging from busy markets overflowing with crafts and novelty gift ideas to local malls and exclusive designer stores.

Of the five centres that feature in the itineraries, the main cities of Auckland, Wellington and Christchurch offer the most diversity. International clothing labels vie with local names of quality such as Thornton Hall, Susanne Gregory, Keith Matheson, Expozay and Barkers Men's Clothing. Budget-priced chains around the country include Glassons and Katies for women, and Hallensteins for men.

The main cities and the resort towns of Rotorua and Queenstown are also well stocked with stores filled with traditional crafts and souvenir products.

What to buy

Woollens

New Zealand is one of the world's major wool producers, and experienced manufacturers take the raw material right through to quality finished products. Handknitted, pictorial chunky sweaters from naturally-dyed wool or mohair are ideal if you are heading back to a northern winter. Innovative wall hangings created from home-spun yarns make another worthwhile purchase.

Leather

The same farming heritage has led New Zealand to develop an extensive leather industry fed by skins from local tanneries that are amongst the world's best. Soft polished lamb suede is turned by craftsmen into superb designer dresses and jackets. Other excellent products include wallets, bags, leather jackets, jerkins, full-length evening coats, country clothes, gloves and the big, warm, fleece-lined 'Ugg' boots.

Sheepskin

With over 60 million sheep, it is little wonder that sheepskin is a major shopping attraction. Full-fleece sheepskin rugs in their natural state, or processed are innovatively used for car-seat covers, floor rugs, mattress covers and baby rugs.

Woodwork

New Zealand is blessed with unique and beautiful timbers including the native kauri and rimu. Crafts-people are skilled at turning these timbers into works of art. Bowls and trays, or purely decorative polished wood pieces make ideal gifts.

Maori Carvings

The time-honoured skills involved in Maori carvings has been passed down from one generation to the other. Carv- *Kauri woodwork* ings usually tell stories from mythology and often represent a special relationship with the spirits of the land. The spiritual forces of Maori carving are imbued on items of both wood and bone. Intricate objects from Maori carvers can command very high prices, but replicas available in most tourist centres provide an attractive (and cheaper) option. Bone carvings are often turned into symbolic neck pendants.

Greenstone

Highly prized for traditional and spiritual reasons, greenstone (New Zealand jade) was formerly used by the Maori in ornaments and weapons. It is now used in jewellery and decorative items such as the Maori *tiki* (a pendant worn to bring good fortune). You can watch the stone being worked and also pick up some good bargains at greenstone factories in Auckland and on the West Coast of the South Island. The unique and beautiful final product is also widely available in shops all over the country.

Paua

The paua fish (abalone) has been revered by Maori for centuries, not just for its flesh but for its delicate shell. The shell with its opalescent colours is polished and used for jewellery, trinkets and other small ornaments.

Pottery

Pottery is regarded as one of the most developed of New Zealand art forms and local potters are renowned for producing some of the finest ceramic art in the world. Examples of their

A proud potter

Sample our seafood

work can be seen at many crafts shops. While driving, watch out also for road-side signs pointing to a potter's house. It is always a diversion worth taking.

Food

Savour the taste of New Zealand back home with its natural produce. Processed items like local jams, chutney, pates, smoked beef and honey do not need documentation, and make excellent gifts as they are attractively packaged. Indulge yourself with fresh local fruit like strawberries, kiwifruit, tamarillos or stone-fruit. And sample fresh seafood such as oysters, scallops and mussels from harbour-side stalls.

Wines

Wines are a real New Zealand success story. The country's young wines, with their fresh and exciting flavours, are jumping up and demanding attention in the international market. White varietal wines such as Sauvignon Blanc and Chardonnay are consistantly well grown in New Zealand. Call in at local wineries or talk to people in bottle-stores or restaurants. They will be happy to guide you in the right direction if you wish to pick up a bottle or two.

Sports and Outdoor Equipment

New Zealanders love The Great Outdoors so it should come as little surprise that they have developed a wide range of hard-wearing clothing and equipment to match tough environmental demands. With some of the best fishing in the world, it is not surprising to find some of the best tackle. Warm and rugged farm-wear like Swandri bush shirts and jackets are popular purchases, while mountaineering equipment, camping gear and backpacks set world standards. Some items have even become fashion success stories, like the range of Canterbury rugby and yachting jerseys.

Where to Buy

Auckland

The two main markets in this city are: the **Victoria Park Market** (Tel: 309 6911, open daily, Victoria Street West) with a huge range of craftwear and designer men's and women's wear; and the **China Oriental Market** (Tel: 302 0678, open daily, corner of Quay Street and Britomart Place), full of colour, variety and bargains with an Asian flavour. **Queen Street** offers a wealth of up-market shopping opportunities for those ready to part with their money.

Duty free shopping is concentrated in the downtown area, while some of the best boutiques are found in the suburbs of **Takapuna**, **Parnell** and **Newmarket**.

Rotorua

Shopping is concentrated along the city's main drag, **Tutanekai Street**. There are a variety of souvenir stores specialising in Maori crafts, sheepskin and leather products at prices perhaps a little better than the main cities. Boutique shopping is limited.

Wellington

The best stretch of boutique shopping is along **Lambton Quay**. There is plenty of variety, including the best selection of top quality clothing shops in the country. For crafts and antiques – buying or browsing – you can indulge in a good couple of hours wandering along **Tinakori Road** or **Upland Road**.

Christchurch

Cashel Mall is the best bet for inner-city shopping, **Merivale Mall** at Papanui Road has some fine boutiques, and the **Arts Centre** market, Worcester Street, is best for crafts.

Browsers and buyers alike at the Victoria Park Market

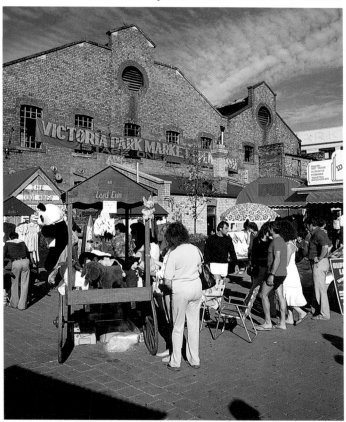

Eating Out

Traditionally, New Zealand has been guilty of resting on the laurels of its agricultural heritage too much. Meals were simple, based on the 'meat and three vege' philosophy inherited from the UK and lacking inventiveness, but this has very much changed, especially in the major cities. European influences are now strong in top New Zealand restaurants where you can expect to find the best of French and Italian cuisine, supplemented with a wine list of impressive local vintages.

Chefs have increasingly been turning to Asia and the Pacific for inspiration to expand their menus, and there has been a surge in the number of ethnic Thai and Japanese eateries of world standards opening around the country.

Another trend is towards a healthier use of foods. More and more restaurants have vegetarian meals available on their menus, and full vegetarian restaurants are becoming more prominent. Traditional New Zealand meat cuts are now leaner and cooked in less calorie-laden ways. Still, the focus always remains on fresh New Zealand produce.

Naturally, fish is abundant and of superior quality. Varieties include delicious freshwater salmon, sole and flounder, snapper and orange roughy. Whitebait – tiny minnow-like fish – dipped in batter and deepfried into crispy fritters are another delicacy.

Look for road-side stalls selling succulent crayfish, or splash out and try one if you find it on any menu (usually the most expensive dish). New Zealand green-lipped mussels are a popular item judging by the number of restaurants offering them on their menus. In the summer you will find mussels tossed on barbeques and cooked in a tangy sauce as they are steamed open. Oyster varieties include the Pacific oyster, the rock oyster and the famed Bluff or Stewart Island oyster. Unfortunately, the catch has been down in recent years for the latter variety, but if you can get your mouth around any of these morsels, your life may never be the same again.

Meat, of course, is writ large on most menus in New Zealand. And you know you will be getting value for money. Lamb, hogget (one-year-old sheep) and mutton is often found tra-

Succulent salmon

Meat is plentiful and features prominently in New Zealand cuisine

ditionally roasted and served with a dollop of mint sauce, but more and more chefs are presenting meat in innovative ways. Beef comes in a variety of cuts but steaks like T-bone or filet mignon are found on most menus.

Vegetables are widely grown all around the country, and varieties you may be offered include aubergine (eggplant), silver beet (Swiss chard), asparagus and beans. The New Zealand pumpkin is tops as is the local kumara (sweet potato).

Fruit like kiwifruit, strawberries, raspberries, boysenberries and rock and watermelons are the mainstay of dessert menus, supplemented with rich ice creams and the fluffy, white dessert known as pavlova. When you are out driving, look for the fruit stands, which in the north sell tropical and citrus fruits and apples, and in the south apples and stone-fruit.

Recommendations

Tearooms abound in New Zealand, serving light lunches of generally fried food, and snacks of pies, sandwiches and rolls washed down with weak tea or coffee. Major cities tend towards cafe and brasserie type establishments, upping the octane rating of the coffee, throwing away the deep-fryer, and stylising the food. Like everything, you get what you pay for. Restaurants open around 6pm and

Tangy kiwi fruit is found everywhere

last orders can be had around 10pm. Note that BYO (Bring Your Own) indicates a restaurant licensed for the consumption, and not the sale of alcohol. A three-course meal without drinks for one person is categorised as follows: Expensive = NZ$50 and above; Moderate = NZ$25–NZ$49; Inexpensive = less than NZ$25.

Auckland

JURGEN'S RESTAURANT
12 Wyndham Street
Tel: 309 6651
A wonderful award-winning restaurant situated in a historic building. Crystal and silver settings and a menu that specialises in fresh New Zealand seafood and meats cooked flambé style. *Expensive*

CIN CIN ON QUAY
Ferry Building, 99 Quay Street
Tel: 307 6966
Fashionable restaurant with the focus on fresh New Zealand produce including venison and Canterbury lamb. Linked to a bar, it offers a complete night out. *Moderate*

SAILS
The Anchorage, Westhaven
Tel: 378 9890
A great setting, overlooking the yacht harbour and Auckland Harbour Bridge. The outstanding location is matched by the quality of its seafood. *Moderate*

THE FRENCH CAFE
210 Symonds Street
Tel: 377 1911
Located up-town and featuring French-style cuisine using fresh New Zealand produce. Decor is casual and elegant. Courtyard dining in the summer. *Moderate*

Rotorua

AORANGI PEAK RESTAURANT
Mountain Road, Mt Ngongotaha
Tel: 347 0046
A fine dining restaurant with superb views and a cuisine highlighting the best of New Zealand produce. *Expensive*

POPPY'S VILLA
4 Marguerita Street
Tel: 347 1700
Great hospitality in this elegant Edwardian villa. Relaxed atmosphere and quality New Zealand meat and seafood. End your meal with the rich New Zealand ice-cream dessert. *Moderate*

Wellington

GRAIN OF SALT
232 Oriental Parade, Oriental Bay
Tel: 384 8643
Quality dining featuring innovative cuisine and fine New Zealand produce. Intimate atmosphere and a good wine list. *Expensive*

TAJ WINE BAR AND RESTAURANT
Corner of Cambridge Terrace and Kent Terrace
Tel: 385 1974
A unique setting, housed in a former public convenience. Spicy vibrant food and a friendly, welcoming atmosphere. A must-try is the seafood gumbo. *Moderate*

IL CASINO
108–112 Tory Street
Tel: 385 7496
This long establised restaurant is famous around Wellington, and for a good reason too. With its sumptuous Italian food and evocative atmosphere, it makes for a super night out. Look for the mural of a Venice street scene on the outside of the building. *Moderate* to *Expensive*

Striking a pose

The Dux de Lux

BRASSERIE FLIPP
103 Guznee Street
Tel: 385 9493
Old building with continental atmosphere enhanced by live jazz at weekends. A great choice for casual dining. *Moderate*

THE ORIENTAL THAI
58 Cambridge Terrace
Tel: 801 8080
One of the many good, inexpensively-priced Asian restaurants in Wellington. The setting is not the most exotic, but the chefs are content to let the good food do the talking. *Inexpensive*

Christchurch

IL FELICE
56 Lichfield Street
Tel: 366 7535
A very popular Italian BYO restaurant. The owners, Paulette and Felice, pride themselves in recreating the full Italian experience, from fresh pasta right down to the passionate ambience. You are in for a special treat if Luciano is waiting tables. *Moderate*

THE BRIDGE RESTAURANT
128A Oxford Terrace
Tel: 366 9363
Warm and intimate atmosphere combines with delicate French-style cooking of New Zealand produce. A central location across from the Avon River. *Moderate*

SIGN OF THE TAKAHE
Dyers Pass Road, Cashmere Hills
Tel: 332 4052
Fine dining in a castle on the Cashmere Hills. Combines a unique atmosphere – baronial yet intimate – and magnificent cuisine to compliment the choice location. A selection of fine wines. *Expensive*

THE DUX DE LUX
Corner of Montreal Street and Hereford Street
Tel: 366 6919
Laid-back vegetarian dining in a restaurant/bar complex that overflows with activity. Try a brewed-on-the-premises beer while you are there. The garden bar is a treat, winter or summer. *Inexpensive*

Queenstown

HMS BRITANNIA
The Mall
Tel: 442 9600
Hearty meals in a fun nautical setting. Not surprisingly the menu is inclined towards seafood. The HMS *Britannia* is licensed, so be careful if you are made to 'walk the plank'. *Moderate*

ROARING MEGS RESTAURANT (BYO)
57 Shotover Street
Tel: 442 9676
Fine dining in an original goldminer's cottage dating from the late 1800s. Flambé cooking is a speciality. *Moderate*

THE COW
Cow Lane
Tel: 442 8588
A small place with big ideas about its pizzas. Located just behind the Bank of New Zealand. It is often very crowded, so you may have to wait. *Inexpensive*

Nightlife

New Zealand's nightlife options can vary considerably, depending on the size of the place you are visiting. In small towns do not be surprised to find little more than a humble pub. Pubs are a great New Zealand social tradition: enter one and you will seldom find yourself short of conversation or an opinion. In recent years many city pubs have become more sophisticated, with 'boutique' beer brewed on the premises, brasserie-style food and up-market chrome and steel furnishings.

The main cities have a variety of cosmopolitan dance clubs with a predominantly young clientele, and late night bars for incurable insomniacs. In resort towns like Rotorua and Queenstown, nightlife tends to centre around the better hotels, or restaurants and bars with late licences.

Drama, dance and classical music performances take place in the larger cities, with international acts usually held at the town hall or major convention venues such as Auckland's Aotea Centre, Wellington's Michael Fowler Centre and the Christchurch Town Hall.

A Queenstown dance club scene

Auckland
Pubs/Bars

THE SHAKESPEARE TAVERN AND BREWERY
61 Albert Street
Tel: 373 5396
Both upstairs bars feature good live band music, and also quiet corners and couches for conversation. Downstairs public bar is noisier and filled with locals.

THE OAK AND WHALE
269 Parnell Road
Tel: 309 6096
Mediterranean-style decor, featuring tavern, grill and restaurant. Attracts a youngish clientele.

THE EXCHANGE TAVERN
99 Parnell Road
Tel: 373 2531
Has three bars to suit your different moods – the casual Safari bar popular with a young crowd, the Long Room filled with 25- to 35-year-olds; and the upmarket Intermezzo wine bar for sophisticates.

Clubs

THE STAIRCASE
17 Albert Street
Tel: 377 0303
The pick of the nightclub scene for the young be-with-it crowd. Trendy but unpretentious. Plays funky music hot off the charts.

STANLEY'S NIGHTCLUB
192 Queen Street
Tel: 309 0201
An old-style dance club, almost verging on the dowdy but popular with an older clientele.

ALFIES
5 Century Arcade, High Street
Tel: 379 6096
Very young patrons and a strong gay presence.

Live Theatre

THE CENTRAL THEATRE
Lower Greys Avenue
Tel: 377 1755
Where regular professional productions take place.

THE GALAXY THEATRE
Corner of Albert Street and Customs Street
Tel: 302 0095
A mix of drama, dance and comedy.

WATERSHED THEATRE
90 Customs Street West
Tel: 358 4028
The venue for innovative theatre, dance and music.

Aotea Centre at night

Classical Music

AOTEA CENTRE
Aotea Square
Tel: 307 5050 (for information)
Also features drama and dance performances.

Rotorua
Pubs/Bars

CHURCHILL'S
426 Tutanekai Street
Tel: 347 1144
An English style bar, as its name suggests, with a good selection of beers and wines from all over the world— and cider on tap.

CARDS
Fenton Street
Tel: 348 7139
An upmarket cocktail bar – perfect for pre-dinner drinks – located at the Sheraton Hotel.

Clubs

ACE OF CLUBS
8 Ti Street
Tel: 346 2204
Open from Wednesday to Saturday nights for dancing. Loud music, a little downmarket, but heck, it's a lot of fun.

Wellington
Pubs/Bars

THE BACKBENCHER
Corner of Molesworth Street and Sydney Street
Tel: 472 3065
Polished wooden panels, supplemented by political memorabilia from the Parliament just across the road. A fun bar with a warm and friendly atmosphere.

WESTERN PARK TAVERN
285 Tinakori Road
Tel: 472 1320
One of the oldest pubs in the country. Still young at heart, with a lively atmosphere.

AQUA VITAE WINE BAR
101 Willis Street
Tel: 801 7020
Perfect for a glass of wine in plush, yet relaxed upmarket central city surroundings.

Clubs

ARENA
259 Wakefield Street
Tel: 385 0174
DJs pump out a range of loud and extra loud dance music to a varied crowd.

ECSTASY
Corner of Tory Street and Courtenay Place
Tel: 384 9495
Newish club with all the glamour and trappings has made this club *the* place to be seen dancing.

Live Theatre

BATS THEATRE
1 Kent Terrace
Tel: 384 9507
Top quality theatre and a great fringe festival.

TAKI RUA DEPOT THEATRE
Tel: 384 4531
Known for indigenous and alternative dance and drama.

DOWNSTAGE
Cambridge Terrace
Tel: 384 9639
One of the reasons which make Wellington the country's theatre capital.

Classical Music

WELLINGTON FESTIVAL AND CONVENTION CENTRE
(including Michael Fowler Centre)
Tel: 472 3088 (for information)
Also a venue for dance and drama performances.

Christchurch
Pubs/Bars

THE DUX DE LUX
299 Montreal Street
Tel: 379 8334
Trendy but laid-back crowd drink in either one of the two bars, or outside. Live music with a tendency towards folk and blues.

PEGASUS ARMS
14 Oxford Terrace
Tel: 366 0600
Has a great setting and an outdoor

bar across from the Avon River. The boat parked in its yard makes it hard to miss.

THE LOADED HOG
39 Dundas Street
Tel: 366 6674
A boutique brewery located on the south side of town. A very crowded bar and live band music.

Clubs

THE MINISTRY
90 Lichfield Street
Tel: 379 2910
Plays the hippiest sounds from around the world to the hippiest young crowd of ravers in town. The trendy DJs and crowded bars add to the frenetic atmosphere.

PALLADIUM
Chancery Lane
Tel: 365 7086
This nightclub is located in the city centre, attracting a young and very trendy clientele. The highlight is the long and dark dance floor lit by a pulsating light-show.

EASTSIDE SALOON
203 Hereford Street
Tel: 379 1691
Lots of space and lots of glass to look out of. Music ranging from rock, through funk and disco. Fun and trendy.

Live Theatre

COURT THEATRE
Arts Centre, 20 Worcester Street
Tel: 366 6992
A venue for top class professional productions.

ELMWOOD PLAYHOUSE
Fulton Ave
Tel: 355 9875
An intimate local production house.

Classical Music

THE TOWN HALL
Kilmore Street
Tel: 366 8899 for information on the Christchurch Symphony Orchestra.

ARTS CENTRE
20 Worcester Street
Tel: 366 0989 for information on concerts in the Great Hall.

Queenstown
Pubs/Bars

EICHARDT'S TAVERN
The Mall
Tel: 442 8369
Traditional pub in Queenstown's oldest hostelry; features local musicians.

SOLERO VINO
25 Beach Street
Tel: 442 6802
Queenstown's first and only wine and tapas bar. Intimate atmosphere.

Clubs

THE CHICO'S RESTAURANT AND BAR
The Mall
Tel: 442 8439
Casual cafe-style dining that transforms into a small nightclub featuring live rock and country music.

WESTY'S RESTAURANT AND NIGHTCLUB
The Mall
Tel: 442 8635
Contemporary design married to old stonework gives the place a warm, cosy feel. Cafe-style dining by day and a large dance floor and live music by night.

LONE STAR TAVERN
14 Brecon Street
Tel: 442 9995
Huge portions of Tex-Mex food by day and a wild party atmosphere by night.

Calendar of Special Events

The sunshine and longer days of summer from December through February mean that these months are packed with regular scheduled events. The local councils of the major cities all organise a wide range of activities, including outdoor concerts and family picnic days. There are also a host of sporting events. For specific dates of events, please contact your nearest Tourist Information Centre (see *Practical Information*). The following are a general listing of events.

DECEMBER – FEBRUARY

New Year's Eve: (31 December) This signals the start of extended holidays for many New Zealand families as they generally kick-start the new year in style. Most cities have public parties in their respective centres, with music, fireworks and the traditional singing of the *Auld Lang Syne* at midnight. Celebrations generally go well into the early hours of the new day.
Christchurch Floral Festival: (January/February) This festival of flowers highlights the wonderful flora of Christchurch that give the city its other name, 'The Garden City'. Events include special flower shows and a Miss Floral Competition.
Waitangi Day: (6 February) New Zealand's national day celebrating

the signing of the Treaty of Waitangi. It is a public holiday, and in Waitangi itself (in the Bay of Islands, Northland), an official ceremony takes place at the Treaty House. The spectacular scene of Maori *waka* (war canoes) on the bay make it a special time to visit Northland.
Auckland Anniversary Day Regatta: (1st week of February) See why Auckland is called 'The City of Sails' when literally thousands of yachts of all shapes and sizes take to the water for this annual event.
Marlborough Wine and Food Festival: (February) Special flights are arranged from Wellington and Christchurch to get people to this incredibly popular festival – celebrating the region's wonderful wine and creative cuisine – held in Marlborough at the top of South Island. The festival is usually a sell-out.

MARCH – MAY

Ngaruawahia Maori Canoe Regatta: (March) An annual event near Hamilton that sees the opening of the Turangawaewae Marae (Maori meeting

'City of Sails' – Auckland

house) to the public for the only time each year. The canoe regatta on the Waikato River is an important event in the Maori cultural calendar.

Golden Shears International Shearing Championships: (March) Every year, Masterton (north of Wellington) hosts this unique event where the best of New Zealand sheep shearers gather to see who is the fastest bladesperson in the world.

New Zealand International Festival of the Arts: (March) This biennial event is held in Wellington, and attracts a wide range of world class artists and musicians to the country for performances, exhibitions and demonstrations.

Around The Bays Fun Run: (March) Tens of thousands of people turn out for this friendly run around Auckland's waterfront. It is a truly spectacular occasion.

Royal Easter Show: (March/April) This agricultural and farming showcase in Auckland is the largest of many held regularly around New Zealand at different times of the year. Farming equipment is displayed, stock is judged amidst a carnival atmosphere.

Arrowtown Autumn Festival: (April) Arrowtown, near Queenstown in the South Island, holds a festival to honour autumn each year. There are all sorts of activities and parades arranged but nothing more spectacular than the glorious autumn colours.

Kiwifruit Festival Week: (May) This event held in Te Puke, north of Rotorua, combines a variety of activities around a celebration of the furry fruit that is almost as much a symbol of New Zealand as the flightless bird it shares its name with – the kiwi.

JUNE – AUGUST

Queenstown Winter Festival: (July) Queenstown, in the central South Island, goes a little crazy every year with this festival of winter. Apres-ski activities reach a peak at this time with parades and parties, while on the ski-slopes people dress up to get down. Again, accommodation in Queenstown must be booked ahead during this period.

Ski Fest: (July) Fun and games in and around Taupo and Turangi in the central North Island.

SEPTEMBER – NOVEMBER

Alexandra Blossom Festival: (September/October) The blossoms in the stone-fruit growing area of Central Otago make spring a special time. It is celebrated in Alexandra, an hour by car from Queenstown, with a spectacular parade through town. The festival runs late September through early October.

Cup Carnival Week: (Mid-November) Held in Christchurch, this is one of the highlights of New Zealand's horse racing calendar. Both the New Zealand Trotting Cup and the New Zealand Galloping Cup are competed for within a space of days. Be warned that accommodation is at a premium during this week, so book well ahead of your visit.

Guy Fawkes Night: (5 November) A night of fireworks and fun celebrating an obscure British anti-hero who attempted to blow up the Houses of Parliament.

Practical Information

GETTING THERE

By Air

New Zealand's relative distance from other population centres make air travel the most common form of transport. New Zealand has two major international airports, with Auckland's (AKL) serving as the gateway to the North Island, and Christchurch's (CHC) serving as the gateway to the South Island. Wellington's airport (WLG), with its shorter runway, serves international flights only to and from Australia. All three airports have banking and exchange facilities covering the times of international flights. All have information desks for assistance, and major rental car firms have offices at all airport outlets.

New Zealand's national airline is Air New Zealand. It operates an extensive service throughout the Pacific, linking New Zealand with Australia, Asia (including Japan), the Pacific Islands and the US. It also flies to and from Europe (London Gatwick and Frankfurt) via the US.

Other international airlines serving New Zealand from a variety of countries include Qantas, British Airways, Singapore Airlines, United Airlines, American Airlines, Thai International, Canadian Airlines, Garuda Indonesian, Malaysian Airlines, Continental Airlines, Cathay Pacific, Japan Airlines, Polynesian Airlines, UTA and Aerolineas Argentinas.

Auckland Airport is 22½km (14 miles) south of the city centre. Travel time ranges between 45 minutes and 1 hour depending on traffic. A coach service runs to the city every 30 minutes on the hour and half hour from 7am to 10pm. A taxi to the city is more expensive. A bus links the international terminal with the domestic terminal, or alternatively you can take a trolley and walk the 900m (984yds).

Christchurch Airport is 11km (7 miles) from the centre of the city. Travel time takes about 30 minutes. A bus runs every 30 minutes from outside the terminal. There is also a shuttle bus service and taxis are available.

Wellington Airport is 8km (5 miles) from the centre of the city. Travel time takes about 30 minutes. A coach service runs every 20 minutes, shuttle buses service the major hotels, and taxis are available outside the terminal building.

By Sea

At the present moment, no shipping companies operate scheduled passenger services to New Zealand on a regular basis. Some companies, however, include the country on the itineraries of cruises to the South Pacific islands. For further information, check with your travel agent, or shipping companies such as P&O Lines, Cunard, Royal Viking Line and Sitmar Lines.

TRAVEL ESSENTIALS

When to Visit

New Zealand has four distinct seasons and though temperatures are seldom extreme, visiting at different times of the year offers visitors very different experiences. Summer runs from December to February (Christmas in New Zealand is very often an outdoor event involving a barbecue!); autumn from March to May; winter from June to August; and spring from September to November.

In winter, New Zealand's mountains come to the fore, with plenty of activities available for travellers interested in winter sports such as skiing. If you are a beach or watersports person, then summer is definitely the time to visit. But for general sightseeing, anytime is the right time from spring through autumn.

Visas and Passports

All visitors to New Zealand require passports which must be valid for at least 3 months beyond the date you intend leaving New Zealand

Visa requirements differ, depending on nationality, purpose of visit and length of stay. Check with the New Zealand diplomatic or consular office in your country.

Entry Formalities

New Zealand has three levels of control at all points of entry into the country: immigration, customs and agriculture. Every person arriving in New Zealand must complete an arrival card which will be handed out on the aircraft. Present this to an immigration official with your passport and, if required, a valid visa. Travellers are asked not to bring in foodstuffs, plants and plant or animal products without declaring them to agriculture officials for inspection.

Customs

Goods brought into the country will not be subject to customs duty or sales tax provided they are for personal use and are taken out of the country on departure. Apart from personal effects, visitors are allowed the following concessions free

of duty and tax, provided they are over 17 years: Cigarettes, cigars, tobacco – 200 cigarettes or 250g of tobacco or 50 cigars, or a mixture of all three not weighing more than 250g; alcoholic liquor – 4½ litres of wine (equivalent to six 750ml bottles), and one 1,125ml bottle of spirit or liqueur. Goods up to a total combined value of NZ$700 are free of duty and tax, but goods in excess of this sum may be subjected to both.

Vaccinations

No vaccination certificates are needed to enter New Zealand. However, if within 3 weeks of your arrival you develop any sickness such as a skin rash, fever and chills, diarrhoea or vomiting, you should consult a doctor and tell them that you have recently arrived from overseas.

Weather

The climate ranges from subtropical in the north (in summer this can mean rain showers and humidity) to temperate in the south. Overall temperature variations are limited because of the proximity of most parts of the country to the moderating influence of the sea. However, the rugged countryside does tend to lead to wide local variations within relatively small areas. Inland areas such as the centre of the South Island can be hot and dry in the summer, and icy cold in the winter. Prevailing weather patterns from the west tend to be wetter than from the east, particularly in the South Island where the Southern Alps act as a 'rain shadow' for the eastern regions.

Electricity

Electricity is supplied domestically throughout New Zealand at 230 volts 50 hertz alternating current. Most hotels and motels, however, provide 110-volt AC sockets for electric razors only.

Time Difference

New Zealand is 12 hours ahead of Greenwich Mean Time. Summer Time, where clocks are advanced 1 hour, operates from the last Sunday in October until the first Sunday in March. Because of its position close to the International Date

Line, if you are flying west you lose a day coming to New Zealand.

Clothing

New Zealanders tend to take life casually, and this is reflected in their clothing. They tend to dress informally for most occasions. And in all but the best hotels and nightclubs, fashionably smart clothes (perhaps a jacket for men, trousers and shoes) are all that is necessary.

In late autumn, winter and early spring, you would need to have a warm all-season coat with you, and perhaps gloves and a hat if you are heading inland or to the mountains.

In late spring, summer and early autumn, garments of cotton and cool washable materials are recommended. Shorts and T-shirts are commonly worn but you should also pack a sweater and light jacket. A waterproof jacket is especially valuable in the wetter northern and western regions.

MONEY MATTERS

Currency

New Zealand operates a decimal currency system, with one dollar made up of 100 cents. Coins come in denominations of 5¢, 10¢, 20¢, 50¢, NZ$1 and NZ$2. Notes featuring images of native fauna and famous historical figures come in NZ$5, NZ$10, NZ$20, NZ$50 and NZ$100 denominations. Check the newspapers for the latest rates of exchange.

Banks and Money Exchange

Trading banks are open between the hours of 9.30am and 4.30pm Monday through Friday. Automatic teller machines operate outside these times, but sometimes only until 11pm.

Banking and money exchange facilities

are open at New Zealand's international airports to coincide with the arrival and departure of most international flights. More and more Bureau de Change facilities are opening up to serve the main tourist areas.

Credit Cards

Paying by credit cards is widely accepted throughout New Zealand, with commonly used cards including Visa, American Express, Diners Club and Master Charge. Look out for the logos of accepted cards on the windows of shops, or check with the shop assistant before you start your shopping!

Travellers Cheques

Travellers cheques can be changed at trading banks, large city hotels and many other trading organisations in the main cities and principal tourist resorts.

Goods and Services Tax

A Goods and Services Tax (GST) of 12½ percent is applied to the cost of all goods and services in New Zealand, except for purchases at duty free shops.

Tipping

New Zealanders do not depend on tips for their income and tips are not expected for normal service, even in restaurants and bars or taxis. Tipping for exceptional service, however, should be done at your discretion. Service charges are not added to hotel or restaurant bills in New Zealand.

GETTING ACQUAINTED

Geography

One of the most outstanding features of New Zealand's topography is its diversity. You will see features of the landscape all over the country that remind you of somewhere else, but here, in their unspoiled setting, the features also remain uniquely New Zealand.

The country is situated in the South Pacific between latitudes 34° and 37° South. It is a long narrow country, lying roughly north-south and comprising two main islands separated by a body of wa-

ter named Cook Strait. It is bordered by the Pacific Ocean to the east and the Tasman Sea to the west. Mountain ranges run much of New Zealand's length. A further smaller island, Stewart Island, lies immediately south of the South Island, and the Chatham Islands are located 675km (420 miles) east.

The nearest major land mass to New Zealand is Australia, 1,930km (1,200 miles) north-west.

New Zealand is slightly larger in size than the British Isles. Two thirds of the country are regarded as mountainous and are dissected by swift flowing rivers, deep alpine lakes and sub-tropical forest.

Situated on the Pacific's 'Rim of Fire', New Zealand experiences both volcanic and earthquake activity. Rotorua, in the middle of the North Island, is famous for its intense thermal activity in the form of geysers, pools of boiling mud and springs of hot mineral water.

New Zealand's highest mountain is Mount Cook, in the South Island's dramatic and sometimes impenetrable Southern Alps. The deep south is famous for its fiords – drowned glacial valleys, while spectacular 'Sounds' (large inlets formed from earthquake uplifts) – draw visitors to the top of the South Island. Between, and over all this rugged countryside are fertile soils supporting New Zealand's agriculture industry.

Government and Economy

New Zealand is a sovereign, independent democratic state and a member of both the United Nations and the Commonwealth. The Government is elected every 3 years. The traditional 'first-past-the-post' electoral system, based on the British parliamentary model, has recently been replaced by a proportional representation system called MMP. The two major political forces are the centre-right National Party and the centre-left Labour Party. A group of minor parties seeking greater influence has joined together under the Alliance banner.

The Government's leader is called the Prime Minister, and the Head of State is the Queen of New Zealand, Her Majesty Queen Elizabeth II, usually represented in New Zealand by a resident Governor-General.

New Zealand is often thought of as a farming country. Indeed, wool, meat and dairy products contribute significantly to its export earnings, though the agriculture sector employs less than 10 percent of the workforce. New Zealand is a member of the Cairns Group of agriculture exporting countries pressing for trade reforms in the sector. There are significant natural resources in the country, of which the energy-related – notably natural gas and coal – are particularly abundant and have been heavily developed.

Pressing noses and making friends

People and Population

New Zealand has a population of about 3.4 million, mostly of British descent but with the largest minority (about 10 percent) being Maori of Polynesian origin. The most densely populated area of the country is the northern half of the North Island. About three-quarters of the population are in the North Island, with 25 percent living in the Greater Auckland urban area.

New Zealanders are also sometimes called 'Kiwis' after the flightless bird that is the country's unofficial national symbol (not after the small furry fruit that also shares the Kiwi name!) You may also hear the term *pakeha* which is Maori for Europeans.

GETTING AROUND

Car

With New Zealand host to so much natural beauty, driving offers one of the best ways to see much of the country. The standard of roads is generally high. Multi-lane motorways, however, are limited in their extent – reserved for providing immediate access to and through the major cities. Instead, single-lane highways are the norm. While traffic on them is generally light by European standards, the winding and narrow nature of some stretches of road means you can only go as fast as the slowest truck! So do not underestimate driving times. Despite an open road speed limit of 100kph (60mph), your average driving speed over a long haul trip is more likely to be around 80kph (50mph).

Documents: Drivers and hirers of cars must have a valid licence which can either be a current New Zealand licence, International licence, or one issued in Australia, Canada, the UK, US, Netherlands, Switzerland, Fiji, South Africa and Germany. Check with your travel agent or New Zealand Embassy or Consulate before leaving.

Rules of the Road: The legal speed limit on open roads in New Zealand is 100kph (60mph), while the speed limit in built-up areas is usually 50kph (30mph) – but watch for signposts. New Zealand's signs are based on internationally recognised driving signals, so you should have little difficulty understanding them. We drive on the left, give way to traffic on the right, and give way to right-turning traffic if we are turning left. The wearing of seat belts is compulsory.

For more detailed information, ask for a booklet on driving in New Zealand from a tourist information office.

Car Hire: If hiring a car, you would be wise to book in advance. Major international firms such as Avis, Hertz and Budget offer good deals for pre-booking, and can have the cars waiting for you at most New Zealand airports. If you have not pre-booked, tourist information desks at most New Zealand airports can direct you to other operators to fit your budget. Note that the minimum age for renting a car is 21.

Maps: Detailed road maps are available at bookstores and service stations. Reciprocal membership arrangements may be available between the Automobile Association in New Zealand and foreign motoring organisations. Check it out in advance because AA offices have a wide variety of maps and general information available for travellers.

Taxis

There are taxis available throughout the country, 24 hours a day. Check the Yellow Pages of your local phone book for a number, or ask the staff at your hotel or motel for assistance. Taxis charge an initial flag-down rate, or a call out fee, in addition to charges for per kilometre travelled.

Air

New Zealand's three main domestic air carriers are Air New Zealand (head office, Tel: 09-379 7515), Ansett New Zealand (head office, Tel: 09-309 6235) and Mount Cook Airline (head office, Tel: 03-348 2099).

Domestic airfares may seem rather expensive (for example, a standard Auckland-Christchurch one-way fare is NZ$330) but there are plenty of deals around for flying in off-peak times, or for booking ahead from overseas.

Resort areas of New Zealand are served by Ansett and Air New Zealand's subsidiary company, Mount Cook. Mount Cook links the gateways with the Bay of Islands, Rotorua, Taupo, Nelson, Mount Cook, Queenstown, Wanaka, Te Anau and Milford Sound with a variety of aircraft ranging from Hawker Siddley 748 turbo-prop aircraft to small Cessnas. Their service has a charm all of its own.

Pilots often open up the cockpit to passengers so you can get the best possible view of some of the country's finest scenery. Check out Mount Cook's Kiwi Air Pass offering travel once only in each direction over the airline's entire scheduled network. Pass holders also qualify for a wide range of discounts on flightseeing services, ski planes and coach tours.

If you are pushed for time you would be advised to make at least two or three internal flights because of the length of the country, so check out the best deals with your travel agent.

Bus

Major cities all have extensive local bus services for getting you out and about economically. Check with information offices for details of how they operate. Have coins ready, as you usually pay on entering.

Coaches operate scheduled services on a connecting network throughout the country. It is advisable to reserve seats on coaches with a travel agent, especially if travelling during holiday periods. The main operators are InterCity (head office, Tel: 09-270 5463), Mount Cook Line (head office, Tel: 03-348 2099) and Newmans (head office, Tel: 09-309 9738).

Ferry

The North and South Islands are linked by modern ferries operated by the Inter-Island Line (head office, Tel: 04-498 3999). The ferries sail between Wellington and Picton and carry passengers, vehicles and freight. There are at least three sailings a day, both ways, with the crossing taking about 3 hours. Several fast ferry services have recently begun operating. Check with your local tourism office for information.

HOURS AND HOLIDAYS
Business Hours

Business hours are generally Monday to Friday 9am–5pm. Most stores and shops are open Monday to Friday 9am–5.30pm, and Saturday 10am–1pm. Many also open for one late night a week (till 9pm), usually on Thursday or Friday, and some stores open on Sunday. In tourist areas and resorts, shops are invariably open on Sundays and evenings.

Banks are open Monday to Friday 9.30am–4.30pm.

Bars, pubs and taverns open Monday to Saturday from 11am and close around 11pm. Nightclubs usually open their doors 7.30–8pm and close around 3am.

Public Holidays

1 January: New Year's Day
6 February: Waitangi Day
April/May: Good Friday
April/May: Easter Monday
25 April: Anzac Day
First Monday of June: Queen's Birthday
Last Monday of October: Labour Day
25 December: Christmas Day
26 December: Boxing Day

Also, each province has a holiday to celebrate its anniversary. The dates are: Northland and Auckland, 29 January; Taranaki, 31 March; Hawke's Bay, 20 October; Wellington, 22 January; Marlborough, 1 November; Canterbury and Westland, 1 December; Otago and Southland, 23 March. The holiday is tagged on to the nearest weekend to these dates.

ACCOMMODATION

New Zealand has a wide range of accommodation to suit all budgets. Value for money is generally good in all categories. As well as standard hotel and motel accommodation in central locations, other options include 'farm-stays' where you are looked after on a New Zealand farm, or a stay at an exclusive lodge. Both offer unique holiday experiences. For farm-stay information contact Rural Holidays New Zealand (Tel: 03-366 1919, or write to PO Box 2155, Christchurch). The New Zealand Tourism Board has a detailed

booklet on the lodges of New Zealand, or you may access a dozen of the finest ones through the Select group (Tel: Toll-free 0800-44-1098).

It is advisable to book all your accommodation in advance. This can either be done through a travel agent, through an office of the New Zealand Tourism Board, or at information centres in all major centres for a small fee and a deposit.

A useful guide to a wide range of accommodations is the Tourism Board's *New Zealand, Where to Stay Guide* published in association with the New Zealand Automobile Association and available from NZTB offices throughout the world.

An approximate guide to current room rates (standard double inclusive of tax) is: *$* = below NZ$90; *$$* = NZ$90–179; *$$$* = NZ$180–250 and *$$$$* = above NZ$250.

Auckland

THE PAN PACIFIC HOTEL
Mayoral Drive
Tel: 09-366 3000
Top class, top-of-the-line facilities in mid-city Auckland location near the Aotea Centre. Superb teppanyaki restaurant and bars. *$$$$*

THE REGENT, AUCKLAND
Albert Street
Tel: 09-309 8888
Located in downtown Auckland, one block away from Queen Street. Luxury accommodation with efficient service, a great brasserie and a swimming pool. *$$$*

GRAFTON OAKS MOTOR INN
Grafton Road
Tel: 09-309 0167
Walking distance to central Auckland and close to the Domain. Clean and tidy. Good value for money. *$$*

Luxury lodge-style accommodations

MON DESIR MOTOR HOTEL
144 Hurstmere Road, Takapuna
Tel: 09-489 5139
On Auckland's North Shore, 20 minutes' drive to city centre. Close to beautiful Takapuna Beach. Spacious pool and barbecue area. *$$*

THE RAILTON TRAVEL HOTEL
411 Queen Street
Tel: 09-379 6487
Aging central city budget hotel but with enthusiastic service. *$*

Rotorua

SHERATON ROTORUA
Corner of Fenton and Sala streets
Tel: 07-348 7139
Strategically placed between Whakarewarewa and the city centre. Immaculate rooms and top class service. Wonderful courtyard area with pool and hot pool. Try the private spa grottos. *$$$$*

QUALITY RESORT LAKE ROTORUA HOTEL
Eruera Street
Tel: 07-347 1234
Ask for a room overlooking the Polynesian Pools and Lake Rotorua. You get a great view from the balcony. Friendly staff and good facilities including gymnasium and pool. *$$$*

REGAL GEYSERLAND
Whaka Road
Tel: 07-348 2039
Million dollar view over Whakarewarewa Thermal Reserve, and opposite golf course. Facilities a little tired, but being renovated presently. Helpful management and staff make you feel welcome. *$$*

PRINCES GATE HOTEL
1 Arawa Street
Tel: 07-348 1179
Old colonial-style hotel recapturing bygone era. Near Government Gardens and Polynesian Pools. *$$*

TRAVELLERS PACIFICA LODGE
13 Fenton Street
Tel: 07-348 5998
Small, basic but friendly operation at Lake end of Fenton Street. Self-contained

units. Good base for lakefront walks. Mineral plunge pool and spa. $

Wellington

PLAZA INTERNATIONAL HOTEL
Wakefield Street
Tel: 04-47 3900
Immaculate modern facilities with good views from spacious rooms. Good mid-town location near Michael Fowler Centre and the waterfront. Burbury's restaurant on the top floor offers fine silver service dining. $$$$

JAMES COOK CENTRA
The Terrace
Tel: 04-499 9500
Top management and service in this landmark central city hotel. Handy for Hutt motorway, and the best city shopping. One of the first grand hotels built in Wellington but it has kept up with the times. Joseph Banks restaurant and wine bar is a popular spot. $$$

QUALITY INN ORIENTAL BAY
73 Roxburgh Street
Tel: 04-385 0279
Located just out of the city centre but in a spectacular part of town, giving views back over the city skyline. Walking distance to Mount Victoria lookout. $$

TINAKORI LODGE BED AND BREAKFAST
182 Tinakori Street
Tel: 04-473 3478
Close to rail, Botanic Gardens and restaurants in historical Thorndon area. Scrumptious breakfast buffet. $

Christchurch

PARKROYAL CHRISTCHURCH
Corner of Kilmore Street and
Durham Street
Tel: 03-365 7799
Magnificent location on Victoria Square in the central city. Immaculate rooms,

spacious corridors and top class amenities. $$$$

NOAHS HOTEL
Corner of Worcester St and Oxford Terrace
Tel: 03-379 4700
Opposite Avon River and Information Centre. West facing rooms have unsurpassed views over the city towards the Southern Alps. Well maintained facilities and good service. $$$

QUALITY INN
Corner of Durham Street and
Kilmore Street
Tel: 03-365 4699
Modern, modular designed hotel with clean and bright functional rooms. Good location opposite the Parkroyal and near the Town Hall. $$

THE GEORGE HOTEL
50 Park Terrace
Tel: 03-379 4560
A low-rise development but on a great site across the road from the Avon River and Hagley Park. Nice willow-shaded rooms with balconies. Ten-minute walk to the city centre. $$

WINDSOR PRIVATE HOTEL
52 Armargh Street
Tel: 03-366 1503
Bed and breakfast style accommodation in an old Victorian villa. Share facilities, basic, but good. Central location. $

Queenstown

NUGGET POINT
Arthurs Point
Tel: 422 7630
Rated as a 'lodge' with sporting facilities including tennis and squash. The setting is Nugget Point's glory, with balconies and the indoor/outdoor swimming pool overlooking the Shotover River. Luxury at a surprisingly good rate. $$$

QUEENSTOWN PARKROYAL
Beach Street
Tel: 442 7800
Aging, though well-kept tiered hotel rising back off the road opposite Queenstown's steamer wharf. The rooms are

The Sheraton Rotorua

very comfortable and feature balconies with a spectacular view. *$$$*

GARDENS PARKROYAL
Marine Parade and Earl Street
Tel: 442 7750
Modern hotel on lakefront 200m (219yds) from city centre. Spacious and welcoming foyer gives a hint of the spacious and welcoming nature of the rooms. Management and staff are top class and unobtrusive. *$$$*

QUALITY INN QUEENSTOWN
Corner of Adelaide Street and Frankton Road
Tel: 442 7940
Good value for money. Located at the start of town as you come in from the airport. Some of the rooms offer lake and mountain views. Nice and friendly staff. *$$*

MCPHEE'S HOTEL
28 Rees Street
Tel: 442 7400
Central budget-priced option in a restored old building that dates back to 1863. Plenty of character. Full-facility rooms available as well as backpacker bunks. Right in the middle of the action. *$*

HEALTH AND EMERGENCIES
General Health
New Zealand's cities and towns have excellent public water supplies and tap water is always safe to drink. Visitors, however, should not drink unboiled or untreated water from lakes and streams.

There are no snakes or dangerous wild animals in New Zealand. Sandflies are prevalent in some areas, but these can be effectively countered using insect repellent.

Medical and Dental Services
For non-emergencies, full instructions on obtaining assistance are printed in the front of telephone directories.

Hotels and motels normally have individual arrangements with duty doctors for guests' attention, and they can also assist you in finding a dentist.

New Zealand's medical and hospital facilities, both public and private, provide a high standard of treatment and care. It is important to note that medical services are not free to visitors (except as a result of an accident), so you should buy adequate medical insurance.

Pharmacies
Pharmacies or chemists are generally open from 9am to 5.30pm weekdays. Some also open on Saturday mornings and for one late night a week. Most major cities also have Urgent Dispensaries which are open overnight and through the weekends.

Emergencies
Dial '111' for emergency calls to police, fire or ambulance services.

New Zealand suffers only isolated incidences of serious crime. However, petty crime is a problem. Take precautions to secure and conceal your valuables at all times, and never leave them in a car.

Police
To report a crime, contact your nearest Police Station. Your hotel or motel will be able to assist you in this. Otherwise, consult a phone book. New Zealand police generally do not carry weapons. You should find them approachable and helpful. Do not hesitate to stop and ask them for assistance or directions.

COMMUNICATIONS AND MEDIA
Post
Post Offices generally open Monday to Friday from 9am–5pm. In many areas, postal services and stamps are also available from stores or other outlets.

Telephone

Phone calls made from public telephones to the local area (free call zone) cost 20¢ per minute. There are a mixture of coin-operated machines (that take 10¢ and 20¢ coins) and card-operated machines. Cards can be obtained from most bookshops.

When calling within New Zealand, dial 0 before the city code: Auckland (9); Wellington (4); Christchurch and Queenstown (3). To call abroad, first dial the international access code, 00, then the country code: Australia (61); France (33): Germany (49); Italy (39); Japan (81); Netherlands (31); Spain (34); UK

(44); US and Canada (1). Dialling codes for other areas in New Zealand and overseas can be found at the front of the telephone directory. If using a US credit phone card, dial the company's access number given: AT&T, Tel: 000 911; MCI, Tel: 000 912; and Sprint, Tel: 000 999.

Media

Mass circulation daily newspapers either in the morning, or morning and afternoon, are produced in New Zealand's main centres. *The Herald* in Auckland is the North Island's largest circulation paper, while *The Press* in Christchurch is the South Island's largest. There are also local daily papers (mostly evening editions) published in provincial centres and larger towns.

International newspapers can be found in the larger bookstores and outlets at New Zealand's international airports.

New Zealand has three national television channels and several local television stations. There are a variety of AM and FM-band radio stations across the country satisfying a wide variety of tastes. Most New Zealand hotel and motel rooms have radio and television, and in the main centres, many hotels subscribe to the Sky satellite service for international sports and news links.

LANGUAGE

New Zealand has two official languages, English and Maori. Nearly everyone speaks English (with a distinctive, often nasal accent that has New Zealand commonly pronounced 'Nu Zilind'!). New Zealand has adopted standard English grammar and spelling, but has also added some 'Kiwi-isms' to the vocabulary. You may hear, for instance, the word 'grotty', meaning very dirty; or 'chilly bin', a portable cooler used for picnics; or 'grog', for alcohol. The list goes on, and most New Zealanders will offer translations for puzzled looking visitors.

Maori is a language going through a renaissance in New Zealand. It is now being taught in schools and is commonly spoken in some parts of the North Island. The Maori influence is strong in place names, and many words have entered common usage, for example: *pakeha*, meaning a non-Maori; *kia ora*, for hello; *kai*, for food; and *hangi*, a style of Maori cooking.

SPORT

Fishing

The fresh, clear waters of New Zealand have proved to be a fertile breeding ground for a wide variety of native and introduced fish species, to the extent that the country is regarded as something of an anglers' paradise. New Zealand also has some of the best dry-fly fishing waters of the world and skilled guides are available in the most popular areas.

In the **North Island**, the **Rotorua/Taupo** area offers rainbow steelhead fishing, requiring at times heavy gear for the deep lakes. Fishing either side of winter (April/May and September/October) is the prime time for catches, with **Lake Taupo** and **Lake Tarawera** being two of the most popular locations.

Summertime (October to April) fly fishing is available countrywide, with the **Tongariro River**, south of Taupo, one of the best spots in the world.

The **South Island** offers a wide variety of dry fly, nymph streamer or lure fishing for brown and rainbow trout from spring through to autumn. East coast rivers such as the **Rakia, Waimakariri, Rangitata** and **Waitaki** offer superb salmon fishing with the best months being February and March, and the best times very early in the morning.

Fishing licences are available from fishing tackle and sports shops on a daily, weekly or monthly basis, and a special tourist licence is available for a month of fishing throughout the country.

If you are drawn to the sea rather than the rivers, New Zealand again has much to offer. Big game fishing for marlin has a deservedly fine reputation. The best months are from January to May and the Bay of Islands is an accessible base, with ample charter boat facilities. For information on fishing charters and guides, check with tourist information offices in any of the towns and cities.

Skiing

The skiing in New Zealand is superb, and with its season opposite to that of the Northern Hemisphere, it attracts a growing number of 'ski-bunnies' down under each year.

The often rugged New Zealand terrain, boasting some of the highest mountains of the southern hemisphere, offers a wide range of skiing opportunities. On-field facilities are top class, with efficient chairlifts and tows, and modern snow-making facilities on the larger commercial fields.

The two **North Island** commercial ski fields are **Whakapapa** and **Turoa**, both located on the slopes of the active volcano, Mount Ruapehu (296m/9177ft), in the central North Island.

With its diverse and spectacularly varied fare, **Queenstown** is an ideal base for skiing in the Southern Lakes' region. The two largest fields are **Coronet Peak** and **The Remarkables**, both easily reached well within the hour from the resort town. Their slopes face different directions, making them skiable in different weather conditions. A drive of just over 2 hours from Christchurch can get you to the central South Island slopes of **Mount Hutt** (with one of the longest seasons in the country) or **Porter Heights.**

A fantastic experience – verging on the sublime – is heliskiing. In this variation of the sport you are whisked by helicopter to slopes of virgin powder amidst mountains of stunning beauty. From Queenstown you can access the **Harris Mountains**, or the **Tyndall Glacier**, while from Mount Cook you can ski a stunning 13km (8 miles) run on the magnificent **Tasman Glacier**.

For information on Coronet Peak and The Remarkables, as well as skiing the Tasman Glacier, contact Mount Cook (Tel: 03-442 7653).

For general information on skiing in New Zealand, you can obtain a copy of the *New Zealand Ski Area Guide* from of-

Weighing in a blue marlin

fices of the New Zealand Tourism Board (NZTB) in New Zealand and throughout the world.

USEFUL ADDRESSES

Tourist Offices

New Zealand is well served by a network of visitor information centres. You will find desks offering information and booking services at most airports and at more than 60 other prime locations around the country. These include:

AUCKLAND VISITOR CENTRE
299 Queen Street
Tel: 09-366 6888

BAY OF ISLANDS INFORMATION
Marsden Road, Paihia
Tel: 09-402 7426

MUSEUM OF CAVES INFORMATION CENTRE
Main Street, Waitomo
Tel: 07-878 7640

TOURISM ROTORUA
67 Fenton Street
Tel: 07-348 5179

WELLINGTON CITY INFORMATION CENTRE
Corner of Victoria and Wakefield Streets
Tel: 04-801 4000

CANTERBURY INFORMATION CENTRE (CHRISTCHURCH)
Corner of Worcester Street and Oxford Terrace
Tel: 03-379 9629

HANMER SPRINGS VISITOR CENTRE
Main Street
Tel: 03-315 7128

VISITOR INFORMATION CENTRE (QUEENSTOWN)
Corner of Shotover and Camp streets
Tel: 03-442 4100

Cover, Backcover Photography — **Marcus Brooke**, **Craig Dowling** *and* **Marcus Brooke**
Pages 3, 6/7, 14T, 16T, 21, 26T, 26B, 28, 29B, 42T, 45, 46T, 55, 59, 60B, 61, 62, 65T, 65B, 67B, 68, 69, 79, 90
10/11, 13, 15B, 17, 18B, 23B, 24, 33, 37T, 50B, 63B, 64, 75, 78, 84, 86, 88 — **David McGonigal**
30, 36, 37B, 60T, 91 — **Jörg Reuther**
15T, 16B — **Auckland Institute and Museum**
14B — **Terence Barrow Collection**

Senior Desktop Operator — **Suriyani Ahmad**
Handwriting — **V. Barl**
Cover Design — **Klaus Geisler**
Cartography — **Berndtson & Berndtson**